EDWIN ARLINGTON
Robinson

A CRITICAL INTRODUCTION

Riverside Studies in Literature

Riverside Studies in Literature

GENERAL EDITOR · GORDON N. RAY

EDWIN ARLINGTON

Robinson

A CRITICAL INTRODUCTION

Wallace L. Ludwig Anderson

STATE COLLEGE OF IOWA

Houghton Mifflin Company · Boston

NEW YORK   ATLANTA   GENEVA, ILL.   DALLAS   PALO ALTO

To

MARY

HALE

and

WHIT

Preface

Born into a period of shifting values, both in society and in literature, Edwin Arlington Robinson came to maturity just as the transition from the old to the new was being made at the turn of the century. From 1896 to 1935 he produced twenty volumes of poetry, most of it of high quality. Though he was somewhat obscured for a time by some of the more experimental poets of the twentieth century, he has been increasingly recognized as a poet of stature and significance in his own right, and as an important figure in the diverse movement to bring American poetry into consonance with the modern spirit. On both grounds, Robinson's life and work are worthy of study.

Although two biographies and a number of specialized studies of Robinson have been published, there has been no book for the college student and general reader that combines biographical and critical material. Charles Cestre's *An Introduction to Edwin Arlington Robinson* presents a sensitive view of certain aspects of Robinson's work, but it is limited to a discussion of the poet's work to 1927 and has long been out of print. Ellsworth Barnard's perceptive critical study purposely excludes biographical material.

The present volume is designed to bridge the gap by providing a somewhat comprehensive introduction to E. A. Robinson the man, his growth and development as a poet, his major work, and his relationship and contribution to modern American poetry.

Though this book owes much to the work of other Robinson scholars, it also includes the results of my own research and contains new material on a number of topics — for example, the Swedenborgian movement in Gardiner, Robinson's working relationship with Dr. A. T. Schumann, the importance of Robinson's early prose sketches. The picture of Robinson's poetic context, the world of poetry at the turn of the century, also varies considerably from the standard view.

I owe a special debt of gratitude to Mrs. William S. Nivison, Robinson's niece and literary executor, for her warm interest in my work, for providing personal information about Robinson and his family, and for permission to print material hitherto unpublished. I am also grateful to a number of Robinson's friends and associates, some now dead, for granting me personal interviews and, in some instances, access to personal papers: William Stanley Braithwaite, Rollo Walter Brown, H. Bacon Collamore, Chauncey Giles Hubbell, Robert Morss Lovett, John Richards, Rosalind Richards, and John Reed Swanton.

For numerous acts of assistance I wish to thank the staffs of the Colby College Library, the Library of Congress, the Gardiner Public Library, the Houghton Library of Harvard University, the Maine State Library, the Library of the New Church Theological School, the New York Public Library, the Portland Public Library, Princeton University Library, the State College of Iowa Library, and the University of Virginia Library.

I am obligated to John Richards and the Board of the Gardiner Public Library for permission to quote from the manuscripts of Dr. Alanson Tucker Schumann. Robinson scholars in general also owe a debt to Dr. Peter Dechert for setting the Schumann papers in order. Quotations from Robinson's letters to Harry de Forest Smith are reprinted by permission of the publishers from *Untriangulated Stars: Letters of Edwin Arlington Robinson to Harry de Forest Smith, 1890–1905*, edited by Denham Sutcliffe (Cambridge, Mass.: Harvard University Press; copyright 1947 by the

President and Fellows of Harvard College). The poem "The Dark Hills" is reprinted with permission of the publisher from *The Three Taverns* by Edwin Arlington Robinson (New York: The Macmillan Company; copyright 1920 by E. A. Robinson; renewed 1948 by Ruth Nivison).

W. L. A.

Contents

Contents

Chronology

1869   Edwin Arlington Robinson born December 22 at Head Tide, Maine, third son of Edward and Mary Elizabeth Palmer Robinson. His father was a general merchant and lumber dealer; his mother was a former school teacher.

1870   Moved in September to Gardiner, Maine, his home for the next twenty-seven years.

1884–1888   Attended Gardiner High School. Became closely acquainted with Dr. Alanson Tucker Schumann, who introduced him to Caroline Davenport Swan and her little poetry club. At seventeen "became violently excited over the structure and music of English blank verse." Made a blank verse translation of Cicero's First Oration against Catiline. Prose essay "Bores" published in *The Amateur,* school literary journal.

1888–1889   Postgraduate year at Gardiner High School. Studied Horace and Milton.

1890   Robinson's first published poem, "Thalia," appeared March 29 in *The Reporter Monthly* (Gardiner, Maine), which also published his metrical translation "The Galley Race," from Book V of the *Aeneid,* May 31.

1891–1893   Attended Harvard as a special student. Five poems published in *The Harvard Advocate*.

1892   Death of Robinson's father, July. In October Robinson had an operation for necrosis of the inner ear, a disease that resulted in partial loss of hearing.

1893–1896   Returned to Gardiner in 1893, resolved to become a professional writer. Financial situation precarious as a result of the Panic of '93. Wrote a series of prose "sketches" for a projected volume entitled *Scattered Lives*. In collaboration with Harry de Forest Smith, made a metrical translation of Sophocles' *Antigone*. Several poems published in *The Globe, The Critic,* and the *Boston Evening Transcript*. Death of Robinson's mother, November 1896. *The Torrent and The Night Before* privately printed, December 1896.

1897   Left Gardiner for New York, late November or early December. *The Children of the Night* published, December.

1898   Out of funds, Robinson returned to Gardiner, where he stayed from May to November. Spent December at the home of a friend, Arthur Blair, in Winthrop, Maine.

1899   Worked as secretary in the office of President Eliot of Harvard, January to June, a position from which he escaped with "the joy of a liberated idiot." In February he had turned down an offer of $2,000 a year to work on the *Kansas City Star*. Remained in Cambridge until October working on "The Pauper," later called "Captain Craig." In September Robinson's brother Dean died, presumably a suicide, after a long and debilitating illness. In late October Robinson moved to New York.

1902   *Captain Craig* published after being rejected by five publishers.

1903–1904   Robinson employed as a time-checker in the construction of the New York subway, fall 1903 to August 1904, a period of physical and emotional exhaustion.

1905   Given a sinecure as "special agent" in the New York Custom House by President Theodore Roosevelt, a position he held until Roosevelt went out of office in 1909. Roosevelt's review of *The Children of the Night* in *The Outlook,* August 12. *The Children of the Night* reprinted, October.

1906–1913   Robinson's dramatic interlude. Association with William Vaughn Moody, Percy MacKaye, and Josephine Preston Peabody. Devoted much of his time to writing prose plays.

1909   Robinson's brother Herman died.

1910   *The Town Down the River* published.

1911   Spent the summer at the MacDowell Colony in Peterborough, New Hampshire. He returned each summer for the rest of his life.

1914   Received a legacy of $4,000 from John Hays Gardiner. *Van Zorn,* a prose play, published.

1915   *Captain Craig* revised and reprinted. *The Porcupine,* a prose play, published.

1916   *The Man Against the Sky* published. First real critical recognition of Robinson's stature as a poet.

1917   *Merlin* published, first volume in Robinson's Arthurian trilogy.

1919   Celebration of Robinson's fiftieth birthday, *The New York Times Review of Books,* December 21.

1920   *Lancelot* and *The Three Taverns* published.

1921   *Avon's Harvest* and *Collected Poems* published. Awarded Pulitzer prize for *Collected Poems.*

1922   *Collected Poems,* with an introduction by John Drinkwater, published in England. Robinson received honorary Litt. D. degree from Yale.

1923   *Roman Bartholow* published. Trip to England, April-July.

1924   *The Man Who Died Twice* published. Awarded Pulitzer prize.

1925   *Dionysius in Doubt* published. Robinson received honorary Litt. D. degree from Bowdoin.

1927   *Tristram* published. Chosen as the monthly selection of the Literary Guild of America, the book became a national bestseller. Awarded Pulitzer prize.

1928   *Sonnets: 1889–1927* published.

1929   *Cavender's House* published. Robinson awarded gold medal by the National Institute of Arts and Letters.

1930   *The Glory of the Nightingales* published.

1931   *Matthias at the Door* published.

1932   *Nicodemus* published.

1933   *Talifer* published.

1934   *Amaranth* published.

1935   Robinson died, April 6. *King Jasper*, with an introduction by Robert Frost, published.

1

The Poetic Context

After the Civil War, the story goes, in a world of increasing industrialism, materialism, and skepticism, a strong realistic movement arose in the novel and the short story, and to a certain extent in the drama. Literature changed with the times — except for poetry. Poetry, with few exceptions, continued to be of the same old sort — pleasant and innocuous, suitable as space-filler in magazines but unconcerned with the present. Suddenly, however, in 1912 poetry came alive. In 1912 Harriet Monroe founded *Poetry: A Magazine of Verse* and began publishing the work of Ezra Pound, Vachel Lindsay, Hilda Doolittle, William Carlos Williams, Carl Sandburg, Edgar Lee Masters, and a host of other new poets. In 1912 Mitchell Kennerley issued *The Lyric Year,* which, among other new voices, included youthful Edna St. Vincent Millay's prophetic "Renascence." All at once, it seemed, there was a tremendous burst of creativity: the "poetic renaissance" was on; the "new poetry" was born.

Though true in part, such an account obscures as much as it reveals, and part of it is a fiction.

In 1912 Edwin Arlington Robinson was forty-three, with four notable — if not widely known — volumes of poetry already published, the first as early as 1896, sixteen years before the "poetic renaissance" and the "new poetry" had officially begun. Moreover, his poetry, early and late, differs considerably from the work of many who were hailed as "new poets," and he himself disapproved of much that they wrote. Nevertheless, it is within the context of the "new poetry" that we can best approach Robinson and perceive his unique contribution to modern American poetry. But first we must understand what is meant by the term "new poetry."

The "new poetry" constitutes one of the most exciting chapters in our literary history. Its story has not yet been completely written, partly because it is still going on, though by now the main outlines have become fairly clear. But a number of popular misconceptions remain. The term itself is both apt and misleading. It suggests, first of all, that the "new poetry" was quite different from the old, making a sharp break with the past. And this is true — in part. Furthermore, it suggests a single type of poetry, as if all "new poems" could be identified by certain characteristics held in common. And this is false — except in one sense only. Diversity in fact characterizes the "new poetry," especially in the decade or so following 1912. Consider the colorful variety and individuality of the poetry of some of the more notable figures. There was Vachel Lindsay spreading his gospel of beauty, performing his high vaudeville, himself entranced, entrancing audiences everywhere, chanting General William Booth into heaven "with his big bass drum" and the "Boomlay, boomlay, boomlay, boom" of "The Congo." There was Carl Sandburg, son of Swedish immigrants, American to the core, with his hard and tender poems of Chicago and of the prairie, celebrating the "Hog Butcher for the World" and "the shine of the morning star over the corn belt," synthesizing hyacinths and biscuits. There was Edgar Lee Masters, a poetic Dreiser, bringing to life the dead of Spoon River, with their "Tragedy, comedy, valor and truth, / Courage, constancy, heroism, failure" — kith, if not kin, to those in Robinson's Tilbury Town. And this was the "new poetry." There was Ezra the pounderous, with his *Canzoni* and *Ripostes,* singing of Old Provence, "out of key with his time," blasting away from his continental base at an age that "demanded an image / Of its accelerated grimace," taking on all comers, including Amy Lowell, whose generalship was equal to his, marshaling her forces of "Amygists," writing of "Patterns" and "Lilacs." And this was the "new poetry." There was T. S. Eliot, born in St. Louis, educated at Harvard, the Sorbonne, and Oxford, becoming a Britisher, a modern-day John the Baptist, decrying the contemporary wilderness peopled with Prufrock measuring out his "life with coffee spoons," Apeneck Sweeney shifting "from ham to ham / Stirring the water in his bath," and Miss Nancy Ellicott "Riding to hounds / Over the cow-pastures." And this was the "new poetry." There was Robert Frost, "swinger of birches," as New England as maple sugar and stone fences, who "took the road less traveled by." And this, too, was the "new poetry." There were others: Conrad Aiken, Witter Bynner, Hilda Doolittle, John Gould Fletcher, Marianne Moore, Wallace Stevens, William Carlos Williams. And there was Edwin Arlington Robinson, who continued to write, in his own way, as he had been doing since before the turn of the century. It is doubtful that one could find in any literature at any time a more diverse group of poets writing in such a variety of styles. They wrote in free verse, cadenced verse, and polyphonic prose. There were Imagists, Vorticists, and Symbolists. And there were some, like Robinson and Frost, who found traditional forms sufficient for their needs.

Clearly the "new poetry" was no single, unified movement but a multi-faceted one with complex interrelationships. Nor was it limited to the United States. It had its counterpart in England and elsewhere. Nor was the literary movement an isolated one. It is part of a much larger context. Music, painting, sculpture, architecture are also involved. And all are part of an even larger whole. Some day the full and fascinating story will be written. It will be the history of our age.

Fortunately our scope need not be so inclusive, but we must widen our focus somewhat to gain perspective. So far we have noted only the diversity and freedom of expression that characterized the burst of poetic activity after 1912. We have still to consider what caused it and to discover whether, underlying the diversity, there is not after all some common element that gives coherence to the movement as a whole. To do so we must go back to its beginnings.

The idea that the "new poetry" actually began in 1912 is a

literary fiction. It did not begin in 1912 any more than the Romantic Movement in England began in 1798. The very explosiveness of the movement is misleading. It gives the impression of spontaneity, as if the "new poetry" had sprung into existence without any preparation; yet this burst of creativity is evidence that underlying forces had been at work for some time. The "poetic renaissance" was, in a sense, also a culmination. Spontaneous combustion is always preceded by a period of smoldering. The smoldering began during the 1890's, and by the turn of the century there were already sparks and a few licks of flame. An examination of the state of poetry and the critical temper at that time will enable us to see the generative forces that ultimately resulted in the poetic rebirth. It will also reveal some of the conditions that Robinson faced at the outset of his career.

Two closely related ideas were expressed repeatedly in the reviews and comments about poetry during the *fin de siècle*: a general dissatisfaction with contemporary poetry and a desire for a poet. A few citations will indicate the prevailing tenor of thought and intensity of feeling. With obvious irony, a Chicago critic expressed his disdain of current verse:

> True poetry has ever in it the essence of prevision, yet rarely to-day is the poet considered a prophet, even in some other country than his own. He is expected to concern himself with dainty lines to his mistress' eyebrow, odes to a violet or lily of the valley, or sonnets on the loves of the ancient gods of Greece or sunset in the Alps or Rockies. All graver matters touching affairs of state, problems of economics, sociological puzzles, etc., must be left to the practical matter-of-fact folks — or the politicians. What does a poet know about war, or commerce, or tariffs, or the fierce battle for pelf?

Another, disturbed by the Spanish-American War and disconsolate because of "the silence of the prophet-voices that appealed so powerfully to the moral consciousness of the generation before our own," exclaimed: "How we have longed for the indignant words of protest that our Whittier or our Emerson or our Lowell would have voiced had their lives reached down to this unhappy time!" Almost plaintively a Massachusetts critic wrote:

The country needs a poet. England has her Kipling who fights to keep the pirates from stealing his peaches and Alfred Austin who waives his copyright rights for the benefit of whoever care to use his soft poems. We really have no one who can give tongue in rhyme appropriately when events call for expression, or thought bursts the bounds of prose.

Even more striking is the following statement which appeared in the *Atlantic Monthly:*

The dear tradition of a savage world lying wait to pounce upon young poets and crunch their bones was never so visibly contrary to the fact, and therefore never so firmly intrenched in popular belief, as the present day. In reality, national pride feeds itself more and more upon the glories of national literature, and hence it is increasingly necessary if a rising poet does not exist, to invent him. When he does appear, the cakes and ale are all for him. Rostand and Stephen Phillips are living proofs of the sure welcome which awaits a rebirth of poetry.

And a reviewer for the *Outlook* expressed an equally intense sense of expectancy:

The tendency to discern greatness in every newcomer in the field is not, however, a wholly discouraging sign of the times. In this field, as in every other, the wish is the father of the thought; men are looking eagerly for the new poet. . . .

The urgency of these statements and the number of similar remarks made at this time clearly reveal the sense of dissatisfaction and the desire for a poet. Although the reasons for this may not be immediately apparent, they are discernible. A strong nationalistic note is evident, but national pride was not a new thing in American literature. In our young and self-conscious nation the desire for an indigenous literature had been persistent throughout the century. Toward the close of the century this nationalistic feeling was strengthened by the coincidence of a number of factors. In the first place, the nineteenth century "greats" were gone. Bryant had died in 1878, Longfellow and Emerson in 1882, and then in quick succession Lowell, Whitman, and Whittier all within a year. By 1892 they were all dead. Though many had doubts about "the Good Gray Poet" who had sounded his "barbaric yawp over the roofs of the world," the others were highly esteemed. With the passing of these figures, there developed a tremendous sense of loss. There was a vacuum to be filled, and the natural question was "Who will take their place?" At moments of national crisis, particularly during the Spanish-American War, the question became more insistent.

Furthermore, there was a sense of rivalry with England. In 1892 an era also came to an end in England with the death of Tennyson, but there the poetic scene did not appear to be so desolate. In fact, new and exciting figures were appearing on the landscape. Two in particular, though poles apart, attracted special attention: Rudyard Kipling and Stephen Phillips. Kipling's *Barrack-Room Ballads* appeared in 1892, followed in 1896 by his poems of *The Seven Seas*. His poems were filled with the language of the British Tommy and sounded like the twanging "Tinka-tinka-tinka-tink" of the banjo. To call him a successor to Tennyson would be farfetched indeed, but his lines had rhythm and energy and life. Later regarded as "the uncrowned laureate of the British Empire," he was by 1900 the most popular poet in England. Though the literati may have lifted their intellectual eyebrows at Kipling, they could point with pride to Stephen Phillips, whose poetic drama *Christ in Hades* was published in 1896, followed the next year by *Poems,* and two years later by another poetic drama, *Paolo and Francesca*. There was no doubt, they felt, that in Phillips England had once more a major poet. Acclaimed to an extent that Tennyson himself might have envied, Phillips was compared favorably to Sophocles, Dante, and Shakespeare. Again the question was raised in this country: "Whom do we have to match these poetic giants?" And the search for a new poet was intensified.

One more factor played an important part in stimulating the desire for a poet: the calendar. As the 1890's passed, there was a widespread feeling that an epoch was coming to an end. The nineteenth century was old and weary; it was dying. A spirit of restlessness and boredom was felt everywhere. There was a lull, and then a sense of expectancy, especially in the United States, at the approach of the twentieth century. There was a strong sense of beginning afresh with the birth of the new century. This was a new age. And a new age demanded a new poetry.

All these factors — national pride, the loss of the esteemed poets of the nineteenth century, the rivalry with England, and the coming of a new century — contributed to the desire for a new poet. These various forces, however, were not necessarily congruent; they did not point inescapably in one direction. Although the citics agreed in wanting a poet, they disagreed strongly as to the kind of poetry he was to write. What direction should poetry take? Over this question a twenty-year battle was fought, another episode in the recurrent struggle between the ancients and the moderns. It began in the nineties; by 1900 the lines were clearly drawn; and by 1912 the major issues were settled. After that there remained only mopping-up operations and a comic battle among the victorious allies themselves to see who would be in the vanguard.

In order to understand the situation, it is necessary to know what the fighting was about at the turn of the century. To say that it was a battle between the old and the new is not very helpful unless we know what each side stood for. The situation is complicated by the fact that there were not just two sides, but three: two extremes and a mid-position. At one extreme were the ultra-conservatives; at the other, the ultra-moderns. Since Robinson himself spoke out against the kind of poetry the ultra-conservatives favored, and since much of the dissatisfaction with contemporary poetry stemmed from this kind of poetry, let us consider first the ultra-conservatives, the upholders of the status quo.

As early as 1894, when Robinson was in the midst of working out his own philosophic and poetic principles, trying to see clearly the direction he should take, he looked with a critical eye at the poetry that was being published. Everywhere he saw the same kind of thing, a "changeless glimmer of dead gray." In November 1894 *The Critic* published Robinson's plea for a new poet, "Oh for a poet — for a beacon bright." Ironically using the sonnet form to make his point, he called for a genuine poet

> To put these little sonnet-men to flight
> Who fashion, in a shrewd, mechanic way,
> Songs without souls, that flicker for a day,
> To vanish in irrevocable night.

The poem is an indictment of the competent pettiness of contemporary verse, poems put together in such a way as to fulfill the external requirements of form, but empty of spirit and significance, incapable of satisfying the inner requirements of meaning. "What does it mean?" Robinson asked:

> What does it mean, this barren age of ours?
> Here are the men, the women, and the flowers,
> The seasons, and the sunset, as before.
> What does it mean?

The material of poetry is drawn from the ever-present and universal aspects of the human condition. Robinson concluded that it was not the age that was barren but the poets. Yet the idea that the age itself was inimical to poetry was widespread. Paul Shorey, for example, in an article entitled "Present Conditions of Literary Production," in the *Atlantic Monthly* for August 1896, commented that "The century of literary production whose account is vaguely felt to be closed . . . is one of the richest in the annals of mankind." The question now was "how long shall we expect lean years?" Shorey had no doubts about the continuing supply of literature, "if by literature we mean spicy reportorial history of the progress of the world, deftly turned ballads and verses vain, and entertaining fiction." With regard to poetry especially, there was "appalling statistical evidence that, however it be with the taste for reading, the taste for writing verse is not on the wane." But he doubted that great poetry could be produced at that time, chiefly because of the "temporary exhaustion of available *motifs* in the higher fields of literature." By a curious involution of thought he argued that since poets anticipate the knowledge and insights that become generally known at a later time, the poets of the nineteenth century had already treated the ideas of evolution and science that were so disturbing to Shorey's contemporaries; hence, there was at the moment nothing new for poets to write about!

For the reader of his own day, it was neither necessary nor desirable that Robinson identify the "little sonnet-men" he was referring to; in fact, to have singled out a few from the many would have weakened his point. Since these poets and their work are now all but forgotten, it is important for our purposes to identify some of them and to give some illustration of the kind of poetry they wrote.

Robinson's friend and fellow-poet, Dr. Alanson Tucker Schumann, was not reticent about identifying the contemporary poets he disapproved of — at least in the privacy of an unpublished poem. In the following ballade, found among the Schumann manuscripts now in the Gardiner (Maine) Public Library, he gave vent to his feelings:

> How dull and vacant are the times!
>   It seems the singers all are fled:
> And yet we have enough of rhymes —
>   Why then are we dispirited?
>   The words are critically wed,
> And critically chosen too;
>   The thoughts unerringly are sped:
> To wit the Aldrich-Gilder crew.
>
> These poets lounge 'neath painted climes,
>   Or snuggle in a limned bed;
> They deal in dollars, not in dimes —
>   Are praised and pampered, groomed and fed;
>   They nothing know of cellar, shed,
> Or garret where the rain gets through;
>   They only cultivate the head:
> To wit the Aldrich-Gilder crew.
>
> Artificers and clever mimics
>   Of flash and dazzle, flaunt and shred —
> They listen to the larger chimes,
>   But ring the lesser ones instead.
>   The ordered paths of verse they tread,
> Their art is beautifully trim:
>   But ah, how little they have said!
> To wit the Aldrich-Gilder crew.
>
> ENVOY
>
> Are the great minstrels dumb or dead,
>   Who from the hills their trumpets blew,
> That song should be so slightly led? —
>   To wit the Aldrich-Gilder crew.

Although Robinson mentioned no names in his poem, there is no doubt that both he and Schumann were writing about the same dreary situation. In singling out Aldrich and Gilder, Schumann chose two of the leading literary arbiters of the day. Both were editors as well as poets. Thomas Bailey Aldrich (1836–1907) had served as editor of *Every Saturday,* a Boston weekly, for eight years, during which time he established his literary reputation with *The Story of a Bad Boy,* a number of short stories, and several volumes of poetry. He then became editor of the *Atlantic Monthly* (1881–1890), the most coveted post of literary influence and authority in the country. Richard Watson Gilder (1844–1909), who called himself a "squire of poesy," was editor of *The Century,* a leading New York periodical, for nearly thirty years. The opinions of both these men carried a great deal of weight, and since they were associated with prominent journals in the two major publishing centers in the country, minor journals tended to echo their opinions and to follow their tastes in literature. It is amusing to note that Shumann, in another draft of the poem and with possible publication in mind, changed the original refrain to "To wit the modish-modern crew."

Aldrich and Gilder are representative of a much larger group of poets. A glance at the index of a few volumes of the *Atlantic Monthly, Harper's Magazine,* or *The Century* for this period will quickly reveal the names of the "Aldrich-Gilder crew," for the same names appear and reappear in these magazines, and others like them, month after month and year after year in the latter part of the century. In addition to Aldrich and Gilder, the list includes: Henry Cuyler Bunner, Madison Cawein, John Vance Cheney, Ednah Proctor Clarke, Louise Imogen Guiney, Robert Underwood Johnson, Louise Chandler Moulton, Edna Dean Proctor, Clinton Scollard, Frank Dempster Sherman, Marion Couthouy Smith, Edmund Clarence Stedman, Elizabeth Stoddard, Richard Henry Stoddard, John Banister Tabb, Celia Thaxter, Edith Matilda Thomas. The list could be extended. These poets provided the standard fare for the last generation of the nineteenth century. Though there were occasional poems with some individuality, most of them had essentially the same characteristics. They were graceful, melodious, and shallow. Filled with exotic trappings and decorative imagery, they seldom exhibited any fresh perception or depth of feeling. Written strictly in conventional rhymed forms, and with careful craftsmanship, they reflected a make-believe world of dreamy splendor and noble sentiments expressed in stereotyped phrases and archaic diction. Rarely did they come to grips with reality. Here, for example, is a not untypical sonnet by Thomas Bailey Aldrich, published in the *Atlantic Monthly*, May 1894:

Reminiscence

Though I am native to this frozen zone
    That half the twelvemonth torpid lies, or dead;
    Though the cold azure arching overhead
    And the Atlantic's intermittent moan
Are mine by heritage, I must have known
    Life otherwhere in epochs long since fled;
    For in my veins some Orient blood is red,
    And through my thought are lotus blossoms blown.
I do remember . . . it was just at dusk,
    Near a walled garden at the river's turn
    (A thousand summers seem but yesterday!),
A Nubian girl, more sweet than Khoorja musk,
    Came to the water-tank to fill her urn,
    And, with the urn, she bore my heart away!

This strikes one as poetic posturing. And that is exactly what it is. For implicit in the poetry of Aldrich and others of this group, and explicitly stated in the writing about poetry, is an image of the "ideal poet" and his function. The poet is the Keeper of Culture. He should continue the great traditions of the past unchanged. He should write of exalted themes in noble language. His world is the world of Beauty.

The very conservative nature of this concept of poetry may not be immediately apparent; indeed, at first it seems to be a broad concept. Inherent in it, however, is a basic resistance to change that limits poetry in form, subject, and language. Certainly a major function of poetry, and of literature in general, is the transmission of the cultural traditions of a people, but more is involved than just the past. The transmission is *through* literature which is itself an outgrowth of the present and which in turn becomes a part of the living, cumulative tradition. The resistance to change in literature was of course secondary; primarily the resistance was to the vast changes that took place in the social, economic, and political structure of society during the latter half of the century. As these writers viewed the changing scene, they saw these changes being reflected in the literature of the period. The trend began with prose fiction and the local-color movement that became widespread after the Civil War. Though these local-color stories depicted the manners, customs, dress, and language of various sections of the country, the conservatives could not regard them at the outset as really offensive; many of them were charming, quaint, and humorous, and often a nostalgic mist hung over them, veiling the stark reality beneath. Gradually, however, the sentimental trappings of local color dropped off as fiction moved toward greater realism, and the contemporary scene appeared in its natural garb. Novels and short stories appeared which dealt with the everyday life of the common people and were written in their language. It was at this point that the reaction began, even among some writers of fiction who felt that the commonplace was drab and uninteresting, and that Romance was what the story-teller should write about. In the real world cities grew up, with factories and slums; depressions, strikes, violence, and crime occurred. Unsettling ideas were abroad, too: Darwinism, socialism, anarchism, nihilism. And increasingly all of these things were caught up in the net of fiction as realism moved into the darker waters of naturalism. To the conservatives it seemed obvious that life had become vulgarized and language debased.

The contemporary scene, both in life and in literature, was a far cry from the sterling or even "plated-Boston" Culture that had for so long held sway over the land. And where was the poet's world of Beauty? He must create it out of the things that remained: nature, the past, and dreams.

Meanwhile poetry had not remained completely untouched. Dialect poems were on the increase. In 1870 Bret Harte's "Plain Language from Truthful James," popularly known as "The Heathen Chinee," created a stir almost equal to the sensation created by Harte's first local-color story, "The Luck of Roaring Camp." The poem was noted in *Every Saturday* with the following comment:

The familiarity of our poets with gamblers who cheat at cards and who have marvellous powers of versification without a corresponding correctness of orthography must be set down as one of the phenomena of current literature.

In 1871 John Hays's *Pike County Ballads* appeared, in which was recorded the crude but vibrant quality of the frontiersman's life and speech. Dialect poems were not new in American literature. As early as the Mexican War, and again during the Civil War, James Russell Lowell had amused and prodded the nation with the twangy dialect of Birdofredum Sawin and other characters in *The Biglow Papers*. Many of the dialect poems that appeared in the latter part of the century were merely humorous, and their distortions of language were of the kind that largely accounted for the humorous appeal of Artemus Ward. Others, however, were more serious, and more accurate in their rendition of dialect. James Whitcomb Riley, for example, whose folksy poems in Hoosier dialect began appearing in the 1880's, was clearly to be taken more seriously — and he was immensely popular. Straws in the wind at this time, these dialect poems, crude as they were in many instances, gave hints of a change in poetic direction and must have caused a great deal of uneasiness among the Keepers of Culture. Who could tell how far this tendency might go? Look, for example, at Kipling, "a narsty little brute," as Aldrich called him!

Furthermore, some experimentation was going on. Emily Dickinson (1830–1886), a shy New England recluse, recently dead, had carried on a quiet revolt, both in her life and in her poetry, the intensity of which was first revealed in 1890 with the publication of *Poems by Emily Dickinson, Edited by Two of Her Friends, Mabel Loomis Todd and T. W. Higginson.* Written in conventional hymn meters, but with subtle flexibility and a daring use of language and off-rhyme, here were poems to make readers sit up: images glowing with white heat, flashes of penetrating insight; out of her domestic Amherst world, a universe of paradox and surprise. Later the Imagists would look upon Emily Dickinson as a forerunner of Imagism and as one of their discoveries. Forerunner she was, and a greater poet than any of the Imagists, but her poetry did not go unnoticed at the time of publication. *Poems* went through sixteen editions by 1898, and *Poems, Second Series,* published in 1891, was reprinted five times in two years. Favorable reviews appeared in the *Nation, The Critic,* and *Harper's Magazine.* But Thomas Bailey Aldrich, reviewing her *Poems* in the *Atlantic Monthly,* saw only another example of poetic degradation. Her first volume, he wrote, was a "poetical chaos . . . ideas totter and toddle, not having learned to walk . . . a pathetic yearning to be poems." Noticing the lack of perfect rhyme in the stanza

> I taste a liquor never brewed,
> From tankards scooped in pearl;
> Not all the vats upon the Rhine
> Yield such an alcohol!

Aldrich proceeded to improve it:

> I taste a liquor never brewed
> In vats upon the Rhine;
> No tankard ever held a draught
> Of alcohol like mine.

Inability to rhyme was bad enough, but bad grammar alone was sufficient to condemn her: ". . . an eccentric, dreamy, half-educated recluse in an out-of-the-way New England village (or anywhere else) cannot with impunity set at defiance the laws of gravitation and grammar." He concluded with the remark: "Oblivion lingers in the immediate neighborhood." It did, but not for Emily Dickinson.

To Emily Dickinson we are indebted for another poet whose work diverged radically from the conventional poetry of the nineties, for it was after hearing William Dean Howells read some of her poetry that Stephen Crane (1871–1900) began to write his strange epigrammatic parables. Better-known today as a writer of fiction, the author of *The Red Badge of Courage* and the earlier *Maggie — A Girl of the Streets* (rejected as unsuitable for publication by R. W. Gilder), Crane wrote two volumes of poetry, *The Black Riders and Other Lines* (1895) and *War Is Kind* (1899). Though *The Black Riders* was flayed by the critics, it had six printings within a year. Crane's poems were doubly vulnerable at the time: not only did they epitomize his naturalistic outlook, but they were written in free verse. Containing elements of Emily

Dickinson and Walt Whitman, Crane's poems also point in new directions.

As all these forces for change moved on inexorably, the position of the ultra-conservatives became less and less tenable. Small wonder that by the end of the century they found themselves on the defensive. Knowing their attitudes toward poetry, one can understand their dissatisfaction with the contemporary poetic scene and their desperate attempts to maintain the status quo. One can also understand their intense desire for a poet at this time and the kind of poet they were looking for. They were looking for a poet who would re-establish the line of the great tradition of English and American verse, which they thought had been broken by the loss of the older poets of the nineteenth century — the tradition of "noble" and "exalted" verse which they themselves had been attempting to maintain with decreasing success in the face of changing conditions since the end of the Civil War.

It was clear to Robinson, and it was becoming increasingly clear to others, that nineteenth-century poetry had come to a dead end. It was equally clear that twentieth-century poetry must be different from the old. How to be new? That was the question in its simplest form. But more was involved than mere novelty. The old poetry had failed because it had rigidified a set of attitudes and practices that were no longer meaningful; it had turned its back on the new age. The real question was how to make poetry meaningful in the twentieth century. And there was sharp disagreement as to how this was to be done.

Two major positions emerged. One group, rejecting the artificiality and remoteness from real life of much of the poetry of the late nineteenth century, desired to make a complete break with the past and start afresh. They favored poetry based on the material of contemporary life — labor, industry, politics, the machine age — and expressed in contemporary language; they wanted poetry that was definite and strong and that expressed its modernity in free rhythms rather than in conventional rhyme. They opposed poetry that was "literary" and "academic." This group was ultra-modern and militantly anti-traditional. The second group, although in essential agreement with the first group on many points, allowed greater leeway in the choice of subject and form. They were equally interested in definiteness and strength, and in contemporary language, but they put more emphasis on the modern *spirit* than on contemporary material per se. Both groups unquestionably felt that to appeal to the modern mind, poetry should reflect contemporary life. The difference lay in the kind of material that could be used to achieve this purpose and the way it should be treated.

During the early years of the century, there was a spate of poems that dealt with biblical, classical, and legendary subjects. George Santayana, Richard Hovey, Trumbull Stickney, and William Vaughn Moody, among others, all wrote long poems embodying material of this sort. Sharp debate arose as to whether such material had any place in twentieth-century poetry. Special attention was given to Moody's work, for he had established a national reputation as a poet of promise. His work as a whole epitomizes the conflicting tendencies of this period of transition. So much so that in the critical battle that was going on, critics from the three major camps saw in him, for different reasons, the new poet they had been looking for. When *The Fire-Bringer,* a long dramatic poem based on the Prometheus myth, was published in 1904, the critical response clearly revealed the issues involved. A few citations will suffice to illustrate the three critical positions and to define more sharply the difference between the ultra-moderns and those who emphasized the modern spirit.

In the following passage, the ultra-conservative position is evident:

> . . . Mr. William Vaughn Moody's "Fire-Bringer" is surely another bit of encouragement in the direction of a greater and truer literature. Here again is an old subject worked over, Prometheus, the "Fire-Bringer" and Mr. Moody's pen seems to have been dipped in the stolen magic flame. It may seem an exaggerated piece of laudation, yet it forces itself to expression that here is a man who has gone up into the mountains, whose head has been among the clouds, whose spirit has abided in that rare atmosphere wherein all sordidness of earth is purged away. Here is a man who has caught one glimpse of Olympian heights with imagination. . . .

This is typical of the acclaim accorded by those who regarded *The Fire-Bringer* as "a really noble poem upon a noble theme." They saw in Moody another Milton, who would help restore the great tradition. Other ultra-conservatives, those who read the poem with greater understanding, were aware that Moody was doing more than retelling an old story. And for this reason they condemned the poem:

> . . . it [*The Fire-Bringer*] disappoints us because we think that Mr. Moody is wandering in a field in which his great and distinctive gift will not find due exercise. . . . The poet has not that rare mythopoeic faculty which Shelley so wonderfully exhibited in his "Prometheus Unbound," by which the world of mythic presences becomes really consistent and atmospheric for us. The modern spirit and note too often breaks in upon it. . . .

The great tradition, in other words, must not be contaminated by the present.

The ultra-moderns, on the other hand, who had come to regard Moody as the leader in the movement toward a new and modern kind of poetry because of such earlier poems as "The Brute," "The Menagerie," and "Gloucester Moors," found in *The Fire-Bringer* a movement in the opposite direction:

> . . . a poet who at this stirring moment in the world's history steers his bark back into the Brazen Age, and sings us of Stone Men and Earth Women, Prometheus, the stealer of fire, and Pandora, discloses in himself a certain moral cowardice. He evades the hour's issues, and sails on sterile seas.

> . . . A lover to-day does not write his love letters in Assyrian on bricks; no more should poets to-day revert to antique themes, which the ancients themselves exhausted, or try to bind new meanings on old symbols. . . . One longs to urge him to jettison all his cargo of spurious classicism, and to address men to-day with the modern thoughts that are in him.

Here we have the extreme opposite of the ultra-conservative position: the present should not be contaminated by the past.

Illustrative of the modern-spirit viewpoint are the following two comments:

> Despite a recent argument to the contrary in the *New York Times*, such a treatment of an old myth, vitalizing it with a modern inter-

pretation, seems, as Matthew Arnold thought, to justify a poet for going to early sources for his inspiration.

> It will at once be realized that the value of the material must depend upon the success of the author in translating the symbols so that their human truths are brought home to a modern reader.

The debate over the appropriateness of using older material was of great significance, for at issue between the two modern groups was the question of freedom. Both groups wanted to make a break from the inhibiting attitudes and practices of late nineteenth-century poetry, but the position of the ultra-moderns, if carried to its logical conclusion, would merely exchange the servitude of the past for the bondage of the present. In their eagerness to make a complete break from the immediate past, the ultra-moderns found themselves in the position of seeming to deny the entire past, a position which was neither desirable nor possible. By 1912, with the ultra-conservative forces largely silenced, the issue between the two modern groups had been settled in favor of greater freedom in the choice of both subject and form. And it was out of this atmosphere of freedom that the diversity of the new poetry came. Underlying the diversity was a common bond, the one thing that gives coherence to the whole movement: the attempt to bring poetry closer to the spirit of modern times. But there was also the recognition that there was more than one way to be modern.

The widespread interest in poetry that swept the country about 1912, and the dazzling procession of poetic talent that revealed itself in the years following, unquestionably enhanced the reputation of Robinson. As his work became more widely known, his original and important contribution to modern poetry became increasingly clear, both here and in England. In 1913 when Alfred Noyes arrived in this country to give the Lowell Lectures, he singled out Robinson as "America's foremost poet." About the same time, Robert Frost, in England after twenty years of trying unsuccessfully to place his poems at home, sat down to talk about poetry with Ezra Pound, then self-appointed foreign correspondent for *Poetry: A Magazine of Verse.* "It was in London in 1913," Frost wrote. "The first poet we talked about, to the best of my recollection, was Edwin Arlington Robinson." When Frost returned from England in 1915 to find himself hailed as one of the "new poets," it was Robinson whom he most wanted to meet. By 1917 the "new poetry" had produced work of sufficient quantity and quality to make possible an initial summary. Amy Lowell, arch-rival of Ezra Pound and militant proponent of her own brand of Imagism, undertook the task in *Tendencies in Modern American Poetry*. Her awareness of the complexity of the movement and of Robinson's importance are equally evident:

> When people speak of the "New Poetry," they generally mean that poetry which is written in the newer, freer forms. But such a distinction is misleading in the extreme, for, after all, forms are merely forms, of no particular value unless they are the necessary and adequate clothing to some particular manner of thought.
>
> There is a "New Poetry" to-day, and the new forms are a part of its attire, but the body is more important than the clothing and existed before it.

Instead of attempting to catalogue contemporary American poets, she chose to

> . . . consider those few poets who seem most markedly to represent a tendency. A poetic movement may be compared to a braid of woven strands. Of the six poets of whom I shall speak, each is an exemplar, and I think the most typical exemplar of a strand. But one particular tinge is peculiar to all the strands, and that particular tinge is revolt against the immediate past.

For her exemplars she chose two poets who wrote in traditional forms (E. A. Robinson and Robert Frost), two identified with free verse (Edgar Lee Masters and Carl Sandburg), and two Imagists (Hilda Doolittle and John Gould Fletcher). Chapter One she devoted to Robinson.

To Robinson, who had worked alone and relatively unrecognized for so long a time, it came as a pleasurable irony to discover that he was regarded as a leader in the new movement. The growth of his reputation did not come about as the result of any basic change in his poetry; he had been writing in his own original idiom from the outset. Instead, the age had caught up with him. *The Outlook's* comment at the time of Robinson's fiftieth birthday stated specifically the debt that contemporary American poetry owed to him:

With all his subtlety, Robinson has been a pioneer in the movement to break away from those worn-out symbols of expression which have lost the power to transmit thought and emotion to the modern mind. And he has broken away from all that was lifeless in the old while still holding fast to those enduring principles without which poetry becomes like "sweet bells jangled out of tune."

Mr. Robinson's influence has been much wider than the constantly growing circle of his readers. He has influenced to a very great extent the content and form of modern American poetry.

That a major poet should come out of a period of poetic sterility seems little short of amazing. But time and events do not produce a poet. At a time when most other poets had turned their backs on an age they thought devoid of poetry, Robinson faced it squarely, and out of it, with consummate artistry, wrought poems of great profundity. His personal and artistic integrity and his sensitive concern for humanity and enduring values are evident in every line that he wrote. Both his life and his poetry constitute a major achievement. Though Robinson the man is dead, his work lives on as a significant part of our cultural heritage. The story of the man and his work is a fascinating one. It begins in a small New England town shortly after the Civil War.

2

Background and
Early Influences

There was no thought of poetry in the Robinson household on December 22, 1869. Maine winters are cold, and though the white frame house overlooking the Sheepscot River at Head Tide was well furnished and generally comfortable, there was no heat in the bedroom where Mary Palmer Robinson lay in long and difficult labor. Edward Robinson, her husband, fearful of the effects of the bitter cold, had her moved to the living room where she could be warm by the fireplace. It was there that their third son was born. The mother was thirty-six. There was severe hemorrhaging and Mrs. Robinson almost died. She was ill and weak for months, and it was not until six months later, while she was recuperating at the resort town of South Harpswell, with its vistas of ocean and islands, that the boy was named, by lot, Edwin Arlington Robinson. Whether he noticed the white birds "flying, and always flying, and still flying" is unrecorded.

In 1869 Edward Robinson was fifty-one. He was a shrewd businessman, kindly, but practical and active. He was red-faced and bearded, tall, a bit stoop-shouldered, but upright in character. And he had done well at Head Tide. He ran the general store, was banker and postmaster, served as selectman and, for a time, as representative in the state legislature. Moreover, he was an astute judge of standing timber, and it was mainly in the business of buying and selling timber that he had made his fortune of $80,000. One of the reasons for settling at Head Tide was its location. The area was thickly wooded, forty miles inland, and the river was swift: logs could readily be floated down to the towns along the coast. Now it was time to move. Edward Robinson was ready to retire, at least from storekeeping, and his sons needed better schooling than the country school at Head Tide could provide. The oldest boy, Horace Dean, was twelve, Herman was four, and now there was a new son. The move had been planned before the baby was born. In fact, the house had been sold; but because of Mrs. Robinson's weakened condition afterwards, the family had been permitted to stay on for a time.

In September 1870 the Robinsons moved into their new home on Lincoln Street in Gardiner, Maine. It was here that Robinson grew to maturity, and it is here that we must seek to discover, so far as they are discernible, the forces that shaped him both as man and artist. In Robinson man and artist are singularly fused, though the formative influences are intricately complex.

One notion about Robinson must be scotched at the outset: the alleged negative influence of Puritanism on him.

". . . Puritanism, at this late day," wrote Amy Lowell in *Tendencies in Modern American Poetry,* "has resolved itself into a virulent poison which saps vitality and brings on the convulsions of despair. . . . Unless one understand this fact, one cannot comprehend the difficult and beautiful poetry of Edwin Arlington Robinson. . . . Mr. Robinson himself is a strong man, his weakness is his inheritance, that outworn Puritan inheritance, no longer a tonic, but a poison, sapping the springs of life at their source." It is clear that Amy Lowell admired Robinson's poetry, but it is equally clear that she did not fully understand it. Even "The Man Against the Sky," Robinson's magnificent affirmation of faith, she at first mistook as an "emissary of gloom or of despair" until Robinson explained it to her. On the subject of Puritanism, Miss Lowell exaggerated and oversimplified. Puritanism, as it is commonly understood, refers either to a set of theological doctrines known as Calvinism or to a cluster of negative attitudes about morality which are outgrowths of the dogma itself. The theological position is summed up in the ideas of original sin, predestination, grace, and election. In this view, man is innately depraved as a result of the Fall and condemned to eternal damnation; by God's grace the elect are saved, a chosen few only. This is a gloomy outlook for the rest of mankind. The narrow conception of morality derives from the doctrine of the elect. In theory, election rests solely with God; man's merits are no necessary guarantee of salvation. Hence anyone had a chance, though there was no way of knowing who had been chosen; and since it is inconceivable that God would reward the bad and punish the good, the practical thing to do was to be good. Good, however, was defined negatively in terms of avoidance of sin. And since sin was identified with pleasure, especially sensual pleasure, it was but a short step to the condemnation of such things as drinking, dancing, and card playing. In neither of these senses is the term *Puritan* applicable to Robinson. In matters of religion he regarded himself as a liberal. After reading William Cowper's *The Task* in 1894, Robinson wrote to Harry de Forest Smith, ". . . you must be prepared to treat Cowper kindly for his intense Calvinism. His religious reflections are not always pleasant to a modern reader, especially if he is inclined, like you and me, to be liberal in such matters." The Robinsons attended the Congregational church, but its creed, according to Emery Neff, was Unitarian. Nor was there at home any of the suppressive morality associated with narrow-minded Puritanism. The Robinsons served good food and had wine at the table. According to Hermann Hagedorn, Edward Robinson, "at sixty-odd, could still cut a pigeon-wing on the dance-floor to the confusion of the younger generation."

The Puritan tradition is by no means wholly negative. A strong sense of moral integrity, a highly developed conscience, a concern with the inner man, and strength of character, as exemplified in such men as Bryant, Emerson, Hawthorne — and in Robinson — are characteristics of the New Englander and attributable, at least in part, to the Puritan tradition. Robinson's strength, which Amy Lowell clearly recognized, may indeed owe something to this inheritance; but it was not outworn, nor was it a "virulent poison." That there was a poison "sapping the springs of life at their source" Robinson saw even more distinctly than Amy Lowell. Indeed, a large part of his poetry is devoted both to the poison itself and to an antidote for it. But this poison resulted, not from decadent Puritanism alone, but from congeries of forces that piled up increasingly during Robinson's lifetime.

Gardiner, during Robinson's boyhood, was a thriving river community with a population of about 5,500. Situated at the junction of the Cobbossee River and the Kennebec, it derived much of its livelihood from the rivers. The Cobbossee furnished water power for the three paper mills and several lumber mills. There was still a considerable amount of shipping on the Kennebec, though increasingly the Maine Central Railroad was taking the place of the steamships just as they had supplanted the graceful sailing vessels that formerly had come into port at Gardiner. And there was a thriving ice business. Kennebec ice had a reputation for purity. The annual harvest of this "frozen gold" was quite an affair: gougers marked the field, sawyers cut the blocks, men with picks guided it through canals, and chains and hooks hauled the glittering crystal cakes up runways into the icehouses. Later it was sent to New York, Philadelphia, Baltimore, Washington, and to other ports in the south, occasionally to Port au Prince, and possibly even to Mediterranean ports and as far as Calcutta. By 1896, it is reported, the ice business on the Kennebec had grown to such a point that icehouses could store 1,500,000 tons half of this at Gardiner and Randolph. At one time or another, most Gardiner boys and young men, including E. A. Robinson, had jobs on the river during the ice season.

The main business street, appropriately named Water Street, on which were located the two small hotels, the banks, the shops, and the library, ran along the riverfront. In the center of the town was the Common. Today it has a parklike appearance, and in one corner stands a memorial to "A man of heroic character, steadfast purpose, and shining genius, whose poems have kindled in many hearts an undying flame." In those days the poet was unknown and the Common was an unlandscaped grassy area enclosed by a two-rail fence. Clustered about the Common, or nearby, were most of the churches of Gardiner. Nowhere does New England express its solidarity and its individuality more than in the number and diversity of its churches. Gardiner had its proper share: Episcopal, Congregational, Free Will Baptist, Calvinist Baptist, Universalist, and Roman Catholic. The Methodist church was across the river. The Swedenborgians had formerly had a church building, but in Robinson's time they met in the home of Mrs. Swanton. The residential part of the town rose sharply from the river and spread out over the surrounding hills, thinning out into farms in the outlying regions.

Edward Robinson had built his new home on a two-acre lot at the corner of Lincoln Street and Cemetery Road. The two-story frame house was large and comfortable, with an ell at the back and a barn behind. The place where Edwin — or Win, as he was called at home — was to write his first poems was the second-story room with a bay window looking out on a ravine with a small stream that ran along the edge of the property. In the yard there were elm trees, a fruit orchard, mainly apple and cherry, a kitchen garden, and a strawberry patch. Across the ravine dwelt Dr. Alanson T. Schumann, homeopathic physician by profession, poet by preference, a man who was to play an important part in Robinson's apprenticeship as a poet.

Records of Robinson's boyhood are scanty, but the ones we have of those early years, before the shadows fell, give us a glimpse, in Laura E. Richards' words, of a "cheerful and cultivated home" and a world of boyish activities. Edward was a man of "substance and position." He had invested heavily not only in Gardiner industries but also, over a period of years, in real estate in the Midwest. A director of two local banks, he was also a community leader: councilman, alderman, and member of the school board. Robinson's mother, a former school teacher, is described as a "quiet, very sweet-tempered lady" with "satiny skin and delicate peach-bloom coloring." The relationship between father and mother was evidently a close one. Hermann Hagedorn records an event, in the earlier days at Head Tide, that suggests the strength of the tie. Edward Robinson had been elected to the legislature. "He went, but reluctantly, for Augusta was as much as fifteen miles from Head-of-the-Tide; and, after twenty-four hours, sent an urgent appeal to his wife to join him. He could not stand, he said, being without her." Both parents enjoyed music. Mr. Robinson, a fine baritone, liked singing such songs as "The March of the Cameron Men," accompanied by his wife at the piano. In the only extended autobiographical statement that he ever made, Edwin Arlington Robinson referred to his mother and father as "the best and kindest of parents." His first book, *The Torrent and The Night Before,* was to have been a surprise for his mother, but she died just before it was printed. Robinson's second volume, *Children of the Night,* is dedicated "To the Memory of My Father and Mother."

Robinson started school at the age of five, attending first a private primary school in the nearby home of Mrs. Mary Morrell, "a woman beloved and honored by all who knew her, who taught generations of Gardiner children their alphabet and much besides." He attended Mrs. Morrell's school for six years and the public grammar school for two years, and then went on to Gardiner High School.

Since both his brothers were older than he, it was natural that young Win should find his companions among his schoolmates. And with them he engaged in the usual boys' activities. Sometimes the boys were invited to the Robinson home, but the favorite gathering place was at the home of the Swanton brothers, Walter, Harry, and John, both because of its location "on the way from the homes of most of the other boys to the swimming places along the river" and because of the Swanton boys' widowed mother, Mrs. Mary O. Swanton, who was, in the words of her youngest son, "a boy's dream of what a mother ought to be." In an unpublished reminiscential note about Robinson and the Swantons, Harry Swanton wrote: "My mother was one of those women who had rather stand the inconvenience of entertaining her neighbor's children than have her children find their pleasure away from home, who had rather her boys would run the risk of getting drowned by playing around the river than acquire bad habits by loafing around the streets. . . ." He described Win Robinson as "a rather large, awkward boy, not particularly good at any of the boys' sports, though he entered with a good deal of zest into all of them, playing 'three old cats' or 'scrub,' swimming, or taking tramps in the woods." In the summer their play included "swimming in the river at White's Ice House and Bradstreet's Wharf, building rafts out of old railroad ties, playing around on the logs, which in those days lined the river below Gardiner, trips on the river in the row boat my younger brother [John Swanton] had saved up his small earnings and bought, tramps to Nahumkeag Pond after pond lilies and for picnics, etc." In the winter the boys made snowhouses and forts, and there was of course sliding on the hills, Robinson on his beautiful black walnut sled, Hum-Strum, which his father had made for him.

"During his boyhood days," according to Harry Swanton, "Edwin Arlington Robinson probably spent more of his time at our house than at any other except his own." In fact, Win Robinson and Will Atwood "were there so much one year that . . . it seems as if during the summer vacation they could have been at home only about long enough to sleep and get their meals. . . . What influence if any my Mother had on Win I cannot say, but I cannot help but feel that she had considerable on all the boys who used to come to our house." Her influence on Robinson, as we shall see, was indeed considerable.

Life was of course not all play. There were chores to be done around the house, horses to be curried, the garden to be taken care of, the strawberry patch to be weeded. There was studying to be done. And there were quiet times of observation and of reading, times for gaining impressions of the world of reality and of the world of imagination.

One of Robinson's grammar school teachers remembered "The shy and friendly way in which he recognized me. . . . He was a highly sensitive child, looking at the world objectively, for the most part, and quick to observe the humor in everything." These qualities — a high degree of sensitivity, the ability to look at the world, including himself, objectively, and a quick sense of humor — were essential parts of Robinson's character, evident throughout his life to all who knew him, and reflected time and again throughout his poetry.

Robinson, recalling the gay parties in the Robin-
ime of her engagement to Herman, remembered
the background. . . . His father thought he ought
other boys, and would try to induce him to go,
ys to curl up with a book." Harry Swanton also
. memories of young Robinson and books: "During the
latter years, when he was at our house, he was more likely to be
found in the front part of it reading a book, than anywhere else."

Robinson came under the spell of words at an early age. Reading was a part of family life in the Robinson home, and Edward
Robinson had built up a good library which included, among
others, the works of Dickens, Scott, and Thackeray; there was
poetry as well, ranging, as Hagedorn notes, "from Shakespeare to
Mrs. Hemans." Bryant's *A Library of Poetry and Song* was a favorite volume. The family spent many an evening together reading
aloud. Something of the boy's growing interest in books and his
parents' awareness of it has been charmingly recorded by Laura
E. Richards. The parents "watched with deepening, if amused,
interest the development of their unusual child. At five he was
reading *The Raven* to his mother as she sat at her sewing; at seven
he discovered Shakespeare — the sound of him at least; the sense
was to dawn a couple of years later. He and his father never tired
of poring together over Bryant's 'Library of Poetry and Song'. . . ."

With the exception of poetry, Robinson's early reading was the
typical fare of boys of his generation. "When I was young," Robinson wrote to Mrs. Richards, who thought that he was "steeped in
Zola and Hardy" as a boy, "I read mostly Dickens, dime novels
(which cost five cents), Elijah Kellogg, Harry Castlemon, Oliver
Optic, Horatio Alger, Bulwer Lytton, Thackeray, and Bryant's
Library of Poetry and Song." Dickens, though Robinson disliked
"the inevitable Victorian stickiness" of some of his work, was a
lifelong favorite. According to Esther Bates, who for many years
typed Robinson's manuscripts, "Dickens he knew by heart." He
was especially fond of *Our Mutual Friend, David Copperfield,* and
Great Expectations. His favorite novel by far, however, was Thackeray's *Pendennis.* As he grew older his reading interests widened
and deepened, but it was not until the 1890's that he read Hardy
and Zola.

It was poetry that gave him the greatest pleasure. "I was inordinately addicted," he wrote in "The First Seven Years," "to reading the somewhat unusual amount of poetry that was in the house." This predilection for poetry did not go unnoticed. John Swanton, for example, was aware of Robinson's devotion to poetry, and his comments reveal something of Robinson's early interests and attitudes: "By and by we began to hear rumors that Win Robinson liked poetry. Later we heard that he did not like Longfellow, and that was heresy of the first water at that time, for Longfellow headed the list of favorites with old and young. Later I could see why Win took to Tennyson rather than Longfellow, Tennyson being more of a poet's poet. . . ." Swanton, who had a particular liking for Scott's "Lady of the Lake," Moore's "Lalla Rookh," and Leyden's "Mermaids," once told Robinson that in poetry he "loved melodious flow of sound." To which Robinson replied, "You must look out for that." On a later occasion, in the summer of 1891, "We happened to talk about Tennyson and he asked me if I had read 'Locksley Hall Sixty Years After.' When I said I hadn't he asked me if I would like to and when I said 'Yes,' he went indoors and brought out a volume containing it. I opened it and started reading to myself but he said, 'Aren't you going to read it out loud?' 'Oh!' I said, 'I didn't know you wanted me to,' and he exclaimed, 'I hadn't any other idea.' " But by this time Robinson already knew that he was "doomed," as he said, "to the writing of poetry."

He began writing when he was eleven, composing his verses in the seclusion and warmth of the barn or in his room, where, as his sister-in-law recalled, always hung a portrait of Edgar Allan Poe and a picture of Ophelia "hanging her garlands on the willow by the brook." By the time he was fifteen or sixteen he must have been aware of the direction he was to take. Like Milton, Robinson began seriously to train himself for what he later called his "unaccredited profession." Something of the joy and anguish of these early years the poet himself recorded:

> . . . In those days time had no special significance for a certain juvenile and incorrigible fisher of words who thought nothing of fishing for two weeks to catch a stanza, or even a line, that he would not throw back into a squirming sea of language where there was every word but the one he wanted. There were strange and irides-

cent and impossible words that would seize the bait and swallow the hook and all but drag the excited angler in after them, but like that famous catch of Hiawatha's, they were generally not the fish he wanted. He wanted fish that were smooth and shining and subtle, and very much alive, and not too strange; and presently, after long patience and many rejections, they began to bite.

In high school Robinson took the "scientific" course (mainly mathematics, chemistry, typing, stenography, English, and Latin) rather than the standard college preparatory course, which included Greek as well as Latin, a choice that he was shortly to regret. The choice was made not because Robinson had any interest or aptitude in scientific and commercial subjects but because he had assumed, perhaps mistakenly, from his father's attitude that he would not be permitted to go to college, although his brother Dean had recently graduated from medical school and was a practicing physician. Though Robinson did not do well in mathematics, he was "singularly proficient in English and in Latin."

At least one piece of his writing was thought sufficiently good to be included in the school literary magazine, *The Amateur*. It is a short prose essay entitled "Bores," and as far as is known was his first publication. Like most juvenilia, it is of interest not as a model of composition but as an example of its author's turn of mind. It deals with the idea that though civilization has progressed to the point where people no longer are tortured for trivial offenses or differences in religious belief, there are nonetheless obstacles blocking the paths of civilization. Presumably man has advanced to the point where he knows his duty:

Man's duty on this earth is the performance of that which will benefit not only himself, but the community. He should work for his own interest, but at the same time for the public good; he should learn and act accordingly; he should obey the laws and live peaceably; he should mind his own business.

But man in fact does not live up to this knowledge of his duty. There are "slums and narrow alleys of our great cities, . . . signs of degradation on every hand." There are also the bores: gossips, faultfinders, wardheelers, funeral orators. Even literature is petty:

At the present day the world is overflowing with a light class of literature, much of which in material has the same ideas and ends, usually spun to a tiresome length, and containing page after page of description, which is copied almost verbatim into each book the author writes. The excessive perusal of this line of literature blunts the mind of the reader, who in a short time can appreciate no other style. The excessive sale encourages the production, and any one can see the result.

The tone is serious, with a touch of humor and irony.

There is no doubt that Robinson regarded a knowledge of the classics as part of the necessary equipment of a poet. He began his acquaintance with the study of Latin. At school his facility with Latin amazed his fellow students. One of them, with vivid memories of the struggle most of them had had with Virgil's *Aeneid,* recalled that "Win Robinson found it so enthralling that while the class was laboring through a couple of pages each day, he had absorbed the entire story, reading with complete understanding, and by a sort of uncanny instinct, text that he did not trouble to translate literally." This was in 1888. Proficiency in a foreign language is not attained without hard labor, and what this student may not have known is the rigorous apprenticeship that Robinson had already served — an apprenticeship devoted not only to learning Latin itself but also to becoming a master craftsman in the art of poetry. As early as 1886 Robinson was using Latin for this larger end. His own statement of this experience reveals his awareness of what he was striving to achieve:

It was about my seventeenth year when I became violently excited over the structure and music of English blank verse, and in order to find out a little more about it I made — of all things possible — a metrical translation of Cicero's first oration against Catiline, which we were reading in school. It began well enough, and with no difficulty:

> O Catiline, how long will you abuse
> Our patience?

That was easy, and invited me to go on. If it lacked something of the vindictive resonance that we feel in Latin, the fault was not in me but in the English language, for which I was not responsible. So

I went on with it until the whole diatribe, which is not short, lay before me in a clean copy of impeccable pentameters (I thought then that they were impeccable) which looked at a glance very much as an equal amount of "Paradise Lost" would have looked if I had copied it on the same quality of paper. It may not have been poetry, and probably wasn't, but many portions of it had music and rhythm and an unmistakable presence of what is nowadays called a punch — for which Cicero may possibly deserve some credit. It was written and rewritten with a prodigality of time that only youth can afford, with an elaborately calculated variation of the caesura, and with a far more laborious devotion than was ever expended on anything that I was supposed to be studying. When this rather unusual bit of minstrelsy was accomplished, and followed by a similar treatment of long passages from Virgil, I had the profound and perilous satisfaction of knowing a great deal more about the articulation and anatomy of English blank verse than I had known before.

After graduating from high school in 1888, Robinson returned for a year of postgraduate work to study Milton and Horace. At home he also worked on Virgil and continued with his translations. The text of Virgil that Robinson used is now housed, along with the remainder of his library, in the Robinson Treasure Room at Colby College. In the text, in a clear bold hand, Robinson wrote: "Finished Book VII, Jan. 31, 1889." The completion was also carefully noted: "Finished *Aeneid*, May 12, 1889. E. A. Robinson." The blank-verse translation of Cicero's oration Robinson probably destroyed; no copy is known to exist. However, two of the "long passages from Virgil" are extant, and we know from Robinson's letters what some of the others were. In the fall of 1889 he made a translation of Virgil's *Eclogue III*, "Palaemon," which he later "Copied and revised solely for the delectation of A. R. Gledhill," a former high-school friend who had gone away to college. "You will notice," he wrote to Gledhill, "the body of the thing to be in pentameters while the singing match is in Alexandrine couplets — as I wished to retain the appearance of the original as much as possible." Three long passages from the *Aeneid* followed: "The Last Combat," Book XII, lines 788–952, "The Shield of Aeneas," Book VIII, lines 597–731, and "The Galley Race," Book V, lines 104–285. "Great sport but devilish hard work," Robinson wrote Gledhill. "The Galley Race" was finished on April 16, 1890. Six weeks later, on May 31, Robinson had the satisfaction of seeing it in print in a local journal, *The Reporter Monthly,* which had also printed "Thalia," his first published poem, on March 29, 1890.

Though other values accrued from Robinson's classical studies, these technical exercises in blank-verse translation paid manifold dividends. He used blank verse with great effectiveness in his "Octaves" (in *The Children of the Night,* 1897) and in "Captain Craig," "Isaac and Archibald," "Aunt Imogen," and "The Book of Annandale" (all in *Captain Craig,* 1902). He used it again even more expressively in "Ben Jonson Entertains a Man from Stratford" (1915). And in the long narrative poems, which constitute the bulk of his later poetry, from *Merlin* (1917) to *King Jasper* (1935), Robinson used blank verse as a flexible instrument of great power. Indeed, Robinson became one of the few masters of English blank verse.

One piece of translation is of special interest, Horace's "Ode to Leuconoë," for it went beyond an exercise in technique to become a finished poem and part of Robinson's canon. One version was completed as early as May 21, 1891, at which time he enclosed a draft in a letter to Harry de Forest Smith. "You will find it rather too literal for a poetical translation — a little prosy in places," Robinson wrote. "I have not tried Horace since and I doubt if I ever do again. It is too much work for the pay. I have never seen an English translation of Horace that seemed satisfactory to me; perhaps I am over particular, but I doubt if the thing can be done to catch the spirit of the original. Horace is Latin or nothing." Yet in December 1895, while he was working on his first book, he wrote again to Smith, "I have been rebuilding that sonnet translation of Horace's ode to Leuconoë." As "Horace to Leuconoë" it appeared in *The Torrent and The Night Before;* it was reprinted in *The Children of the Night* and was retained in Robinson's *Collected Poems.*

Robinson's close friendship with Harry de Forest Smith was an important one, both for personal and professional reasons. They became acquainted in high school, brought together by a mutual interest in Latin verse. Harry Smith, as Rosalind Richards said, "was born for learning"; he was also, as Robinson remarked to

Gledhill, a man he could "take to his soul." After graduating from high school in 1887, Smith attended Bowdoin College in nearby Brunswick. Later he did graduate work at Harvard and at the University of Berlin. In 1901 he went to Amherst College, where he served for many years as Professor of Greek. When Smith left Gardiner, Robinson missed him terribly, for he felt that Smith was one of the few persons in whom he could confide. During summer vacations, for a number of years, they saw much of each other; at other times they corresponded. Fortunately, Smith had an intuitive sense of Robinson's future stature, for he carefully preserved the letters he received. Now in the Houghton Library at Harvard, these one hundred ninety-one letters are one of the main sources of information about Robinson, especially for the period from 1890 to 1905. Edited by Denham Sutcliffe, they were published, with a few omissions, under the title *Untriangulated Stars*.

Smith both supported and fostered Robinson's interest in the classics. Some time prior to 1894 Smith had suggested that they work together on a translation. In February 1894 Robinson proposed that they "make a metrical translation of the *Antigone*." Smith, Robinson suggested, "might find pleasure and profit in writing out a correct prose version of the play, keeping the Greek spirit as much as possible, and in guiding me in the choice of words and suggestions as to the classical effect of my verses." Robinson, in turn, would make a metrical version which they would publish as a joint translation. Although Robinson was busy with his other writing, he thought "the time and trouble might be a good investment for the practice it would give me in the choice and arrangement of words." Robinson had no knowledge of Greek, but he felt that he had some qualifications for the task: "I know that I have something of the Hellenic spirit in me, and have a pretty good conception of what the word means. I may lack some of the 'serene and childlike joy of life' but I have the spirit of wise moderation and love of classical completeness which, I suppose, is more marked in the later poets of Pericles' time than in the Homeric period." Although the work was never published, Robinson gained much from the experience, much more than practice in "the choice and arrangement of words." He learned a great deal not only about Greek drama but about the art of dramatic construction, a knowledge that was to serve him well in the writing of his long narrative-dramatic works. Indeed, it may be that this experience was partly responsible for his moving in that direction.

Robinson's knowledge of the classics was extensive. Though deep at only a few points, as Fussell pointed out in his study of Robinson's literary background, it included a familiarity with the major figures. In Latin, Virgil and Horace meant most to him, but he also knew, either in the original or in translation, Juvenal, Ovid, and Tacitus. Though Robinson made a brief effort to learn Greek "to get some Greek lymph into his system," he read the Greek authors in translation: Homer, Plato, Aeschylus, Sophocles, Euripides, Aristophanes, and the Greek Anthology. This classical influence permeates the work of Robinson, but his use of it is never sterile nor academic. It was a living part of him, and it became a vital part of his poetry. It gave him a sense of tradition, a broad outlook rather than a provincial one. It affected his thought, his language, and his style. The qualities of moderation and restraint, of objectivity and precision, of order and proportion, coupled with a sense of high purpose and a penetrating insight into and broad sympathy for humanity entitle Robinson to be called, as Cestre has said, "a modern classic."

Though Gardiner was a small town, distant from the literary centers, there were nonetheless a number of people with literary interests. One of these was Dr. Alanson Tucker Schumann, the Robinsons' next-door neighbor and their doctor. Dr. Schumann had a passion for poetry and, apparently, a propensity for women, though he was a bachelor living with his widowed mother. There is some question about his pursuit of women, but there is none about his pursuit of poetry. He had been writing verses since he was twenty, possibly earlier. Everyone must have known of his interest, for he was constantly writing lines and his pockets were stuffed with manuscripts, mostly ballades, rondeaus, villanelles, and sonnets. How and when the doctor discovered that Robinson also wrote poetry is not known, but it could not have been long after Robinson entered high school. The two must have presented a striking contrast: Schumann, twenty-three years older, rather thick-set, with a moustache and short hair, volatile, never at a loss for words; Robinson, getting to be a tall, handsome young man, with thick dark hair and deep brown eyes, shy, keeping his thoughts to himself. Though Robinson at times had mixed feelings about Schumann, they became close friends, and Robinson was indebted to him in a number of ways.

It was not long before the doctor realized that young Robinson was a better poet than he would ever be, and it is to his credit that he sought to encourage and nurture Robinson's poetic development. Encouragement in itself was no small matter, for Robinson "at an early age" saw himself "setting out alone on what was inevitably to be a long and foggy voyage." Schumann once told him, Robinson recalled later, "that I should have to write poetry or starve, and that I might do both — although he did not believe that I should starve, or not exactly. That was encouraging and I have never forgotten it."

It was Schumann no doubt who introduced Robinson to the old French forms which had recently come into vogue. The revival of interest in these forms may be attributed to the Pre-Raphaelites, a group of painters, poets, and artisans in England in revolt against the materialism of their time and the conventions of Victorian poetry; they advocated a return to simplicity and sincerity in art, and found inspiration in the artists and writers of the Middle Ages. Both Dante G. Rossetti and, later, Algernon Swinburne made translations of the ballades of the fifteenth-century French vagabond poet, François Villon. Théodore de Banville's *Petit Traité de Versification Française* intensified the interest in these elaborate forms, and before long Andrew Lang, Austin Dobson, Edmund Gosse, and others were writing ballades, rondeaus, triolets, and villanelles, and spreading the word. Interest was not limited to England. In 1878 Brander Matthews reviewed a volume of Dobson's verse for the *Nation* and subsequently published an article on the history of these forms. Gleeson White's anthology of *Ballades and Rondeaus, Chants Royal, Sestinas, Villanelles, Etc.,* published in 1887, was well known to both Robinson and Schumann. In 1891 Robinson bought two copies of the work, one for himself and one for Schumann. In the introduction White noted that "the Americans have shown themselves more cordial towards the Gallic measures than even our own countrymen. In the popular periodicals of the United States there are more specimens than in our English magazines. . . ." No one was bitten harder by the Gallic bug than Dr. Schumann. Though none of his work was published before 1890, he wrote literally scores of poems of this kind. Constantly revising and polishing his poems, he was, as Robinson observed, "as patient and as careful in his work as a Chinese ivory carver." The doctor's enthusiasm was contagious, and before long Robinson was trying his hand at these exacting forms. With their limited and intricate rhyme schemes and use of refrain, they demanded a nicety of execution, a sensitive adjustment of sound to sense, and a light touch to be successful. Like his practice in translation from Latin, Robinson's experience with these forms provided excellent discipline in improving his facility with various metrical forms and in strengthening his sense of craftsmanship. That there were dangers as well, Robinson became aware as he grew to his poetic maturity, and it is notable that he published no poems of this kind after his first volume. His success in handling these forms may be measured by the examples included in *The Torrent and The Night Before,* particularly "Ballade by the Fire," "Ballade of Broken Flutes" (dedicated to A. T. Schumann), "Villanelle of Change," and "The House on the Hill," the only ones that Robinson retained in his *Collected Poems.*

Schumann also wrote sonnets — hundreds of them. Moreover, he had definite ideas about the sonnet form, ideas that coincide in many respects with Robinson's practices. Although Schumann recognized the Shakespearean and Miltonic forms, he regarded the Petrarchan form as the sonnet *par excellence.* The poet, he thought, should give careful attention to his rhymes:

> These two sets of rhymes [in the octave] should markedly differ as to sound quality. In the minor system, or sestet, there are two or three rhymes and their rhymes are free as to their arrangement. . . . There has been and still is much controversy about the propriety of a rhymed couplet closing the sonnet. We feel that the freedom of rhyme-arrangement in the sestet should be primary; that if the thought demand a rhymed couplet such demand should be respected. The rhymes of the sestet as of the octave should differ as to sound-quality. And all of the rhyme-sets in the sonnet should ring varying peals.

Schumann disagreed with those who regard the sonnet as appropriate for a limited range of subjects only. "The sonnet is a fitting vehicle for the phrasing of every variety of thought," he wrote. It is adaptable to all kinds of moods; "it may do anything which it is asked to do." But above all it must have an organic unity:

> It should be the evolution of a single thought. On the reading of its first verse there should be no doubt in the mind of the reader of its ability to do satisfactorily what it has to do. It should betray no weakening, no uncertainty, no halting, no weariness, no slackness, no unintelligibleness from first word to last, inclusive of both. Its each and every word, as to meaning, music, mission, adaptability in all ways to the words which touch or are near enough to influence should be carefully and jealously chosen and placed. Assonance should be shunned. Intentional inter-rhyming should be avoided, unless it is employed to heighten some certain quality of expression, but such claims rarely occur. Words should not be repeated, as a rule, unless to occasionally strengthen, embellish, or make prominent some thought-link; of course this injunction does not include connectives, prepositions, articles, and the like. . . . We should especially emphasize the sagacious disposing of connectives: many bad sonnets would be good ones if the often recurring small words were more artistically placed. The true poet gives scrupulous attention to these seemingly minor points.

Schumann's insistence on the freedom of scope and the flexibility of the sonnet form stands in striking contrast to the "little sonnet-men" fashioning their trivial sonnets in their "shrewd mechanic way." His awareness of the emotive effects of words and the psychological interplay of structural elements, and his concept of organic wholeness, reveal a rather sophisticated understanding of the nature of poetry. And these were the kinds of things that he and Robinson discussed together.

Among Schumann's poems are a number of sonnets on the sonnet, one of which closes with the lines:

> It is a diamond fixed within a coil
> Of finest gold; it is an opal fraught
> With shifting, fiery, iridescent sheen;

Robinson also wrote a sonnet on the sonnet, which contains a similar gem image in the first two lines of the sestet:

> The sonnet is a crown, whereof the rhymes
> Are for Thought's purest gold the jewel-stones;

The attempt to epitomize the sonnet itself in sonnet form is not
uncommon, nor is the gem image unusual. Rossetti, for example,
one of Schumann's favorite poets, wrote of the sonnet's "flowering
crest impearled and orient." But the similarity between Schumann's lines and Robinson's suggests how close their working
relationship was. There are other similarities. Both wrote poems
on the following authors: Crabbe (many sonnets by Schumann),
Poe, Whitman, Arnold, and Hardy. Schumann wrote "A Ballade
of Decay"; Robinson wrote a "Villanelle of Change." Schumann
also wrote a number of poems on biblical subjects, two of which
Robinson may have recalled in writing "Lazarus" and "Sisera."
One of Robinson's most familiar sonnets, "Credo," begins:

> I cannot find my way: there is no star
> In all the shrouded heavens anywhere;

and ends:

> I know the far-sent message of the years,
> I feel the coming glory of the Light!

Schumann wrote a similar one, which has the following lines:

> The last light glimmers on the last hill's crest,
> The path I tread is bleak, I cannot pray.
> . . . .
>
> I know but this: here all is ominous night,
> With not a star to touch me with its gleam.

Another one opens and closes as follows:

> I cannot find thee — in the dark I grope —
> The skies are void of stars and black with clouds —
> . . . .
>
> Sudden a glory shines where all was drear —
> I clasp thee in the great sun's gracious beam!

With such similarities it is impossible to say who was indebted to
whom. Indeed, it looks as if they set themselves topics on which
to work, and then later compared the results of their individual
poetic efforts.

In addition to his personal encouragement and stimulation, Dr.
Schumann was the means of opening other literary doors for Rob-

inson. During the eighties and early nineties, Gardiner had a small poetry club to which Schumann belonged. The other two members were Henry Sewall Webster, the local judge of probate, and Miss Caroline Davenport Swan, a former high-school teacher who had later studied at Radcliffe. Miss Swan had been Schumann's teacher during his senior year in high school and had given him his foundation in versification. An intelligent woman, with a wide knowledge of art and literature, she was the central figure in the group, which met weekly at her home. One evening Schumann brought Robinson with him, and the young high-school boy became one of the group also. He was then, according to Miss Swan, not more than fifteen years old.

One of the purposes of the club was to "go over each other's verse." This not only gave the young poet a chance for a hearing but was also a means of sharpening his critical faculties. The group also read the current verse in the magazines, thus putting Robinson in touch with contemporary developments in poetry. Frequently Miss Swan read French literature in the original, mainly poetry but some fiction as well. Although Robinson at the time had not studied French, he listened and learned a great deal. Miss Swan would read a passage aloud, translating and commenting as she went along. In the course of time she covered most of the lyric poets of France, early and late, much of Ronsard and Verlaine. And by this means Robinson added another dimension to his literary knowledge.

In an interview with Miss Rosalind Richards in October 1937, Miss Swan, then a very old lady, recalled those early days and her association with young Robinson: "I remember it entirely," she said — "young Win Robinson sat very quiet, listening. He did not talk, but his eyes were very bright, and I noticed that he listened very intently for the whole evening. Yes, sometimes Dr. Schumann brought some of Win Robinson's verse, or persuaded him to bring it himself, and I went over it with him, or we all did. He was learning every day. Our little Club was of great use to him. — But he *was very determined.* He had his own notions; he was one of those persons whom you cannot influence *ever,* he went his own way. — I did not know at all how it would turn out, he was so determined in the way he would work at things for himself — but it turned out very well!"

As long as Robinson remained in Gardiner, he kept up his close association with the group, especially with Dr. Schumann. After Robinson left he continued to correspond with Schumann, each keeping the other informed of what he was doing. But the roles of master and pupil had become reversed. It was Robinson who encouraged Schumann to publish his poems. Although he recognized the limitations of much of Schumann's work, Robinson nonetheless was convinced that the doctor's poems were, as he wrote Harry Smith in 1894, "better than the average magazine stuff." Later, when Schumann wrote about Robinson's eminence as a poet and Schumann's inferiority to him, Robinson replied: "I dont [*sic*] want to hear anything more about your inferiority; for you know as well as I do that I could not produce the equivalent of your ballades if the deposition of the devil depended on my doing so." Schumann for his part, now married and living in a stately home across the river in Farmingdale, came to regard himself as a kind of Robinsonian oracle. "By mouth and by pen," he wrote, "I have, several times, been your interpreter. Should you get consummate eminence I do not doubt but pilgrimages will be made to me from far lands by people who want to know just what you mean in your 'queer' poems." When Schumann finally decided to publish a book of poems himself, he sought Robinson's advice and assistance in finding a publisher. On May 30, 1913, the *Boston Post* published a report of an interview with Robinson that must have given double satisfaction to Dr. Schumann if he saw it. The headline read as follows: "GREAT AMONG POETS HIDES IN MODESTY. Edwin Arlington Robinson, Acclaimed Nation's Greatest Living Poet, Quietly Living in Boston, Unrecognized." Among other poets that Robinson was quoted as having mentioned with approval, Schumann's name appeared as one who "has a peculiar genius for writing ballads and rondeaus in the French form." When Dr. Schumann died in 1918, Robinson, with characteristic generosity of spirit, wrote an article for the *Boston Evening Transcript,* in which Schumann's poems had been appearing for twenty-five years, in praise of "the singularly polished and accomplished verses of this competent, though unostentatious New England poet." And in 1930, in "The First Seven Years," Robinson, at the height of his career, made public acknowledgment of his indebtedness to his "old friend and neighbor, Dr. A. T. Schumann." "As I shall never know," he wrote, "the extent of my indebtedness to his interest and belief in my work, or to my unconscious absorption of his technical enthusiasm, I am glad for this obvious opportunity to acknowledge a debt I cannot even estimate. . . . If he had cared as much about 'the numerous ills inwoven with our frame' as he did about the metrical defects and tonal shortcomings of the major and minor English poets, he would surely have been a most remarkable doctor; as it was, I am sure that he was one of the most remarkable metrical technicians that ever lived, and an invaluable friend to me in those years of apprenticeship when time, as a commodity to be measured and respected, did not exist."

The years immediately following high school were for Robinson years of shadows lengthening into darkness. His father, always a man of energy and physical vitality, was over seventy; now he was deteriorating physically, wasting away, slowly dying. His condition was worsened by the affliction of his eldest son. Dean, the brilliant young doctor so much admired by all, and especially by his youngest brother, had graduated *cum laude* from medical school in 1881. After three years in Gardiner, he had moved his practice to Camden on the coast. Always on call, whatever the weather or season, his practice included the neighboring islands, frequently heavy with fog mixed with sea-spray. Fatigued from overwork, he suffered from sinusitis and neuralgia; the excruiating pain he suppressed with morphine, and within three years he became addicted. He practiced two years at Alna; then, in 1889, he returned home to Gardiner, where he struggled with decreasing success against a demon that would not be downed. His career as a doctor was shattered.

The only bright spot in the family, seemingly, was Herman. In 1884, at nineteen, he had been appointed assistant cashier at the Gardiner Savings Institution, where he gained increasing respect for his business acumen, especially in deals involving real estate. In 1886 he became the bank's western representative; he travelled through the Midwest engaging in land speculation, and finally settled in St. Louis, where he attracted some attention as a bold and imaginative investor. Edward Robinson, who had proudly watched this son, so much like himself, follow in his footsteps, gradually turned over his financial affairs to him. Back east in

1888 to raise funds for the construction of an elevated railway in St. Louis, Herman visited Gardiner. At Capitol Island, where the Robinsons rented a summer cottage, Herman met the lovely and popular Emma Shepard. Apparently as bold in love as in business, he easily won out over the local swains. Engaged, he journeyed back to St. Louis to pursue his business affairs and to buy a house before returning for the wedding. Herman and Emma were married in Farmingdale, across the river from Gardiner, on February 12, 1890. Shortly afterward, Herman set out once again for St. Louis, this time with his bride and with high hopes of making a fortune, unaware of the approaching national financial crisis. Win Robinson remained at home. He was needed there.

His position was a difficult one. He spent his time doing chores, tending the garden, playing checkers with his father for hours at a time, lifting him in and out of bed. He was lonely and longed for the companionship of someone his own age. Smith, Gledhill, and the three Swanton boys had all gone off to college. Ed Moore, who with Gledhill and Robinson had comprised a "League of Three" in high school, had a job and was engaged to be married. Although Robinson did odd jobs from time to time, he did not have a regular job. Nor did he really want one. He read a great deal, worked at his writing, and wrote long letters to his friends about the good times they had had together in high school, about his reading, about his hopes and ambitions. "My time is now pretty well taken up with farming," he wrote Smith, "and I am raising giant harvests of cucumbers, cauliflowers, onions, and God knows what more, in the prolific garden of my mind. That is the only garden in which I have succeeded in raising anything thus far during my life, but I have hopes that I may plant a seed before long that will take root and bring forth something, if no more than fifty cents a week, provided I am to some extent contented with the soil." He knew the job he wanted to do. But he knew, too, that he wasn't yet ready. He was sensitive about his age and his apparent aimlessness, and was angered when someone asked, as they occasionally did, "Well now, Robinson, what do you intend to do?" A visit to Harry Smith at Bowdoin in the fall of 1890 stimulated Robinson to think about the possibility of taking a special course at Harvard. "The experience of a year among new forms and faces" would do him "a world of good in more ways than one." But there were hindrances. His father's attitude toward college had not improved, especially after what had happened to Dean, and if Robinson did go, who would take care of things at home? A painful earache forced a decision. At Dr. Schumann's suggestion, Robinson went to Boston for an examination, where it was disclosed that he had necrosis of the inner ear. Instant attention and periodic treatments were demanded. Under these circumstances, and at the urging of Herman that Win be given his chance for further education, Robinson was permitted to go. The family would have to manage somehow. In the fall of 1891 Robinson enrolled at Harvard as a special student.

In "The First Seven Years" Robinson, with characteristic understatement, dismissed his stay at Harvard with a single comment: "After two years at Harvard College (1891–1893) where I made several good friends, I returned to my home in Gardiner, Maine. . . ." Robinson went to Harvard to shed some of his provincialism by broadening his acquaintance with the world and to increase his literary knowledge. In both of these aims he attained a modicum of success. He did not expect to shine either as "a society star or as 'one of the boys,'" nor did he. But he did make his way among the students; indeed, on several he made a lasting impression.

At first Robinson was apprehensive about his status as a "special" and about his ability to do the work. Although he did not acquire friends easily, he quickly discovered that there was "remarkably little feeling between the students of different grades." Robinson found the course work difficult at first; he was, as he said, "grievously rusty," and early in November, just before the first midterm examinations, he was "rather blue" and wondered whether the whole thing was not after all just a waste of time and money. Less than two weeks later, however, he wrote to Gledhill: ". . . I feel as if I had always been here, and as if I should always like to stay here."

While he was at Harvard, Robinson lived well; he spent about a thousand dollars a year, a standard of living he would not have again for a long time to come. He worked hard, applying himself diligently, especially to those subjects in which he was particularly interested. His first year's work consisted of Rhetoric and Composition, Anglo-Saxon (which he dropped early in November), Shakespeare, Prose Writers of the Nineteenth Century, and French. During his second year he continued his French and began German; he also took Fine Arts III (Ancient Art), a course in philosophy (mainly logic and psychology), and a course in eighteenth-century literature. The literature courses, as one would expect, appealed to him most; he liked especially the two period courses, taught by Professor Lewis E. Gates, and read widely in eighteenth- and nineteenth-century English literature. Shakespeare taught by the eminent Professor Francis J. Child, who stressed historical and linguistic matters, was something of a disappointment, though Robinson recognized and respected Child's erudition. Professor Charles Eliot Norton's lectures in Fine Arts, however, were "simply magnificent." Norton was, Robinson thought, "by all odds the greatest man in America and I am beginning to realize what a privilege it is to sit within six feet of him three times a week and hear him talk." Robinson acquired considerable facility in reading French but made little headway with German. "I wonder why it is," he wrote to Harry Smith, "that every new German book seems like another language."

Although Robinson did not expect to shine at Harvard, there is little doubt that he hoped to make his friends among the literary group and to make some kind of literary impression, a twin goal in which he was only partly successful. One of the first things he did after his arrival at Harvard was to submit a poem for publication in one of the student journals. Accepted immediately, "Ballade of the White Ship" was published in *The Harvard Advocate,* October 16, 1891. This was followed by the publication of four more poems in the same journal in the course of the year: "Villanelle of Change," "In Harvard 5," "Menoetes," and "Supremacy." However, Robinson's efforts to place his poems in *The Harvard Monthly,* the more serious literary journal, were not successful; nor did he make any friends among the *Monthly* group. The closest he came was a talk with the chief editor. Actually, Robinson had sized up the situation rather accurately very early. In a letter to Smith dated October 18, 1891, Robinson wrote: "I have subscribed for the *Advocate* and the *Monthly,* but I doubt if I ever appear in the latter. It seems to be a medium for airing the work of its editors. . . . However, I think I shall spring something on them pretty soon, to see how it will work." In November he called Smith's attention to a poem in *Scribner's* by William Vaughn Moody. At the time, Moody was a junior at Harvard and one of the editors of *The Monthly,* and his poems appeared in nearly every issue. "I am not acquainted with him," Robinson wrote, "but as soon as I get fairly straightened out, if I ever do, I purpose to make a strong attempt to get in with the *literati* of Harvard. My ballad may help me out a little and it may not." It did not, for a month later Robinson received a visit from Robert Morss Lovett, editor-in-chief of *The Monthly.* The sonnet on Thomas Hood that Robinson had submitted had been "weighed in the balance and found wanting." Robinson had his own opinion of the judgment, but he realized that it was "of no value in this case." Robinson, who usually underplayed matters of personal importance, clearly revealed his feelings in reporting this incident to Smith. He referred to Lovett as "Robert Morss Eliott," identifying him with the president of Harvard, Charles W. Eliot; Lovett was "perhaps the leading spirit of Harvard outside of athletics"; Robinson "felt honored to receive a call from him, being a Special and a first year man at that. . . . If I succeed in getting in with such fellows as that, college life will prove most agreeable."

Though Robinson went his own way and was often lonely with the inner loneliness that is both the burden and the strength of many sensitive people, he always had a few choice friends about him. He needed friends and cherished them; most of his close friends were friends for life. There were times, later, when he became dependent on friends for food and shelter, but in his own way Robinson always gave in return, and there were usually others who were dependent on him. Although Robinson did not get in with the *literati* at Harvard, he found companionship with a number of students who banded together under the name of the Corncob Club. In addition to Robinson, the group included Mowry Saben, the central figure, in revolt against practically everything conventional, who later became editor of the San Francisco *Argonaut;* James L. Tryon, also from Maine, who was headed for the Episcopalian ministry; George Burnham, a law student, whose feet had been amputated, and to whom Robinson was especially drawn; Shirley E. Johnson, later a journalist; George W. Latham, who shared Robinson's interest in Matthew Arnold and who became a professor of English at McGill University; Chauncey Giles Hubbell, headed for the Swedenborgian ministry, a man for whom Robinson had high regard; and Frank Q. Peters, later a public-health worker in Chicago. They met informally in one another's rooms, usually Saben's, to talk and to puff on their corncob pipes. The talk was of politics, religion, literature, and, as Emery Neff noted, on "whatever students include under the fascinating term 'life.'" Sometimes flowing spirits added to their own high spirits.

Boston opened up the world of the theater; it also revealed the drama of human existence in forms and conditions Robinson had not known before. Regularly, usually on Saturday evenings, in company with one or more of his college friends, and occasionally with Dr. Schumann down for a visit, Robinson went into town. After a good meal with wine or a few bumpers of beer, they attended the current dramatic production. Though Robinson was critical of some of the plays ("Cheap farce-comedy is undermining the whole dramatic scheme"), he thoroughly enjoyed himself much of the time. Julia Marlowe, whom he saw at least four times in 1892 and twice in 1893 in a number of Shakespearean productions, particularly impressed him. For a short period, after an evening of theater and carousing, there were visits to some of the "midnight palaces" of Boston's demi-monde. These "anatomical investigations" apparently were concentrated in the early months of 1892.

Boston also whetted Robinson's interest in music, an interest that became increasingly strong. In March 1892, he wrote to Smith: "Rather think I shall be fool enough to pay three dollars to hear Patti in *La Traviata* next Thursday evening — that is if I can get a seat. That is the only grand opera excepting *Trovatore* that ever interested me much." But by December he was writing to Gledhill: "I expect to go home the 23rd, but may stop over one day for the Symphony concert. I am getting to be a fiend for that kind of a thing though my experience is limited. Yesterday afternoon I went to hear Damrosch's orchestra at the Tremont Theatre. . . . Symphonies & grand operas are a perfect revelation to me and I am cursing myself for letting so many go by last year."

By temperament Robinson was reticent, often silent, especially in group gatherings. His friends at Harvard sensed also a note of melancholy. Whenever they touched on anything too personal, "he clammed up," Chauncey Hubbell said. Affairs at home were always in the back of his mind, and his ear troubled him constantly. If anything, the situation at home was worse. In July 1892, after lingering on for so long as an enfeebled shadow of himself, Edward Robinson died. Dean continued to deteriorate. The weeks surrounding his father's death were, as Robinson said, "a living hell." Moreover, his ear, which had to be syringed daily, was frequently painful, and he was fearful that the disease might reach his brain. In October 1892, he underwent surgery; two bones were removed, and though the disease was arrested, the operation left him with partial deafness the rest of his life.

In June 1893 Robinson left Harvard and returned to Gardiner. Of his Harvard experience he wrote to Smith: "I have seen things that I could not possibly see at any other place, and have a different conception of what is good and bad in life." And almost a year later, berating himself for lost opportunities while at Harvard, he summed it all up in the statement "my life is infinitely larger for my going there."

3

Toward a
Philosophy and Poetics

The years 1893 to 1904 were for Robinson years of tragedy and of discouragement; they were also years of growth and triumph. There is no paradox here, for it was out of tragedy and in the face of discouragement that Robinson attained mastery of himself and his art. His basic convictions, philosophic and poetic, were forged in fire. Firmly established by the time of the publication of *The Children of the Night* in 1897, they were extended and given fuller embodiment in *Captain Craig,* 1902.

Robinson returned home just as the uncertain economy of the country collapsed in the Panic of '93. For a number of years there had been a growing uneasiness, punctuated by sporadic strikes and riots. In July 1892 a major steel strike occurred in Pennsylvania, followed by a walkout of railroad switchmen in Buffalo, and then by a strike of coal miners in Tennessee. By the summer of 1893 the situation had reached panic stage: gold reserves fell, banks closed, businesses failed, unemployment was widespread. It was one of the most disastrous industrial depressions in the history of the country. And Herman Robinson, in St. Louis, where he had invested heavily in real estate in what turned out to be the wrong section of town, was caught in the downward plunge. Possibly betrayed by some of his associates, he suffered losses, not only of his own money but that of his Maine partners and of the Robinson family as well. Blaming himself for the catastrophe, he broke under the strain and turned to alcohol for support. For the next few years Emma and her two small daughters, later a third, stayed in Farmingdale, though she spent an increasing amount of time in the Robinson household as the family situation worsened. Herman apparently was away from home much of the time, his alcoholism becoming more acute.

First Dean, and now Herman. What of himself? The threat of failure was constantly with Robinson. He felt that the townspeople regarded him as a failure, and he more than anyone else knew how little he had achieved. There were increasing pressures to take a job, to go into business as his father and Herman had done. It is one measure of Robinson's courage and integrity that he chose the most difficult course — and the sanest: to stick to his writing. To do otherwise would be to fail. On October 1, 1893, Robinson wrote to Smith:

> . . . on dark, dull Sundays like this I find it [hard] to be cheerful and optimistic, and everything else that a useful man should be in order to fill his place in nature to the satisfaction of himself and his dear friends who feel so much for his welfare. I am half afraid that my "dear friends" here in Gardiner will be disappointed in me if I do not do something before long, but somehow I don't care half as much about the matter as I ought. One of my greatest misfortunes is the total inability to admire the so called successful men who are pointed out to poor devils like me as examples for me to follow and revere. If Merchant A and Barrister B are put here as "ensamples to mortals," I am afraid that I shall always stand in the shadow as one of Omar's broken pots. I suspect that I am pretty much what I am, and that I am pretty much a damned fool in many ways; but I further suspect that I am not altogether an ass, whatever my neighbors may say. I may live to see this egotistic idea exploded, but until that time comes I aim to hug my own particular phantoms and think as I like.

It was in such a mood as this that Robinson composed his sonnet "Dear Friends." In words of gentle humor that sharpened the irony, he contrasted their idea of success with his:

> Dear friends, reproach me not for what I do,
> Nor counsel me, nor pity me; nor say
> That I am wearing half my life away
> For bubble-work that only fools pursue.
> And if my bubbles be too small for you,
> Blow bigger then your own: the games we play
> To fill the frittered minutes of a day,
> Good glasses are to read the spirit through.
>
> And whoso reads may get him some shrewd skill;
> And some unprofitable scorn resign,
> To praise the very thing that he deplores;
> So, friends (dear friends), remember, if you will,
> The shame I win for singing is all mine,
> The gold I miss for dreaming is all yours.

The imponderables that make the difference between success and failure were to engage Robinson in many a poem; indeed, the success-failure theme is a major one in his work. And the crux of it is a question of values. The world's measure of success was not Robinson's. He had one talent, he felt, and he must use it. Writing would be his justification for existence. "I shall never be a Prominent Citizen," he wrote to Gledhill in August 1895, "and I thank God for it, but I shall be something just as good perhaps and possibly a little more permanent."

Early in 1894 Robinson fell in love. In February he wrote to Smith that he had begun "to tutor a young lady in French preparatory to her entering Wellesley College." The thought that he was "going to be . . . of a little use in this world" made him "rejoice." The young lady was Mabel Moore, the sister of Ed Moore, one of Robinson's high-school classmates. John Reed Swanton recalled her as "a very good looking and thoroughly respectable girl of about medium height or a bit over and tending toward the blonde but not strikingly so." Robinson's period of bliss, if such it was, was brief. On May 1, in a gloomy mood, he reported to Smith: "Perhaps you will understand my feelings a [little] better, and perhaps not, when

I tell you that my French lessons are over. You may interpret this as you like, but I fancy you will not get far out of the way in your conclusions. Anticipation and realization are two different things." A few weeks later, after learning that Smith was engaged to be married, Robinson congratulated him but with ambivalent feelings, partly because he knew that after Smith's marriage their own relationship would be changed, and partly because Smith's engagement aggravated his wounded feelings: "You are engaged to be married, you are happy, and the world and the future look bright in your eyes; I am not (now) engaged to be married, I am not happy, and the world and the future look so dark and gloomy that I look mostly into the past." With prophetic insight, he saw himself "living alone in some city — Boston, most likely — with a friend or two to drop in upon me once in a while, and a few faithful correspondents." By June he had recovered sufficiently to tell Smith that when he came home he would not find Robinson "a broken down wreck or anything of the kind"; his blue mood, he said, was the result of his "failure thus far to accomplish anything or to be anybody in the world" — "rather than," he added, "my separation from the one who is and always will be a part of my daily life. . . ." Robinson never married.

Until the publication in 1965 of Chard Powers Smith's book *Where The Light Falls, A Portrait of Edwin Arlington Robinson,* the episode with Mabel Moore was generally considered to be Robinson's most serious love affair. It is still possible that it was. Smith's thesis, however, is that Robinson's one great love was Emma, Herman's wife. The "Legend of Emma," as recounted by Smith, is based in large part on "a body of almost entirely undocumented evidence" which has descended "by word of mouth" to survivors of Mrs. Herman Robinson, and allegedly derives from her recollections as told to others after Robinson's death in 1935. There is, according to Smith, an "Orthodox Account" and a "Dissenting Account." Apparently E. A. Robinson first met Emma during his last year in high school. He was eighteen; she was twenty-two. She was beautiful, and she appreciated his poetry. Robinson was deeply smitten and may have felt that she returned his affection. During the summer of 1888, when the two were neighbors vacationing on Capitol Island, Herman returned from

St. Louis. Robinson introduced his brother to Emma. "Like a storm with high flying spray," in Smith's words, Herman "went into action, and a few evenings after his arrival pinned Emma into engagement on the dramatic bare pinnacle near the seaward end of the island." According to the Orthodox Account, Emma always loved E. A. Robinson; in this view, her marriage to Herman began with "a superficial infatuation," became a matter of duty, and ended in pity. According to the Dissenting Account, Emma always loved Herman; in this view, though she deeply resented her husband's drinking, her love for E. A. Robinson "was never more than big-sisterly," and her feelings toward Herman were never basically altered. C. P. Smith's view is that "the truth borrows something from each" of the two accounts. Though some of what Smith reports in his book is undoubtedly true, there is also a good deal of conjecture. Until clear-cut evidence is revealed, one must withhold judgment.

On November 22, 1896, a week before the appearance of *The Torrent and The Night Before,* Robinson's mother died. The book was to have been a surprise for her. The circumstances surrounding her death made it a traumatic experience for all concerned. Mrs. Robinson had gone to Boston to visit a friend who was a nurse. In mid-November she returned and complained of not feeling well. A few days later a doctor was summoned; he diagnosed her illness as black diphtheria and refused to return to the house. Dean rallied and did what he could, but his efforts were futile. The undertaker left the coffin on the porch, and Mary Robinson's three sons placed her in it. The minister stood on the porch and read the funeral service through an open window. Since no one would drive the hearse, the brothers had to put the coffin in an express wagon and drive it themselves to the cemetery just a short distance behind the Robinson homestead. After Mrs. Robinson's death, Herman and Emma, with their young daughters, aged six, four, and one, moved in to live with Win and Dean.

Dean's condition worsened after his mother's death. For years he had striven valiantly to overcome his addiction; three times he had undergone treatment at an institution in the hope of being cured. But as the years passed, his brilliant light had grown dim. The purchase of a drugstore in 1897 from the proceeds of Mrs.

Robinson's estate was no doubt a financial investment, but it also served to keep Dean supplied with morphine. "Often bedridden and delirious," according to a member of the family, Dean, in his last years, had to be watched over by an attendant.

A precarious financial situation, two brothers broken, an unhappy love affair, his mother's death — add to this a troublesome ear, eyes that for a time went bad, and Robinson's own sense of insufficiency, and it will occasion no surprise that he spoke of "recent mental disturbances" and a "presentiment" of his own early death. It was against this personal background that Robinson's first two volumes of poems were produced.

One day in the spring of 1892, while Robinson was at Harvard, his friend Latham walked into his room and startled him with a question: "Robinson," he said, "I can't see what this life of ours amounts to anyway. What is the object of it? What are we here for?" "I could not give him a very definite answer," Robinson wrote to Smith, "so I blew a stream of Bull Durham smoke into the air and shook my head. . . . It is not such a foolish question to ask, after all, when we think it over. If we throw aside the gilded Paradise theory, it *is* a question what life really amounts to for more than three quarters of the world." Ultimately Robinson would have to answer Latham's question. And the answer he found had an important bearing both on his life and on his poetry. That he was a proficient craftsman Robinson already knew. He could handle with skill intricate problems of form and meter: he could turn out graceful villanelles, ballades, and rondeaus; he could shape forceful sonnets; and he could manipulate, with some flexibility, lines of blank verse. But this was merely technical skill that any would-be versifier could achieve with practice; it dealt with external matters of mechanics and form which in themselves had no life. To be a poet Robinson had to have something to say. And this was a matter of belief. Moreover, he must put what he had to say in living forms. And this was a matter of art. In short, he had to work out his own philosophy and his own idiom.

It has often been asserted, mistakenly, that Robinson was a pessimist who accepted the naturalistic position that we live in a deterministic and purposeless universe. Van Wyck Brooks, for example, wrote of Robinson that "He could not share the old assurance that life was part of a purposeful plan, much as he wished to share it and almost did so." Robinson grew up in a period of increasing skepticism, at the time of the great debate over science and religion when many people adopted an extremely negativistic attitude toward life. The implications of Darwin's *The Origin of Species* alone seemed to undermine the foundations of religious belief, leaving a jungle world of tooth and claw or a mechanistic world of indifferent forces. Such a view was expressed by the disillusioned Mark Twain, and it pervades the work of Thomas Hardy. Indeed, a deterministic conception of the universe is central in naturalism. But this is not the conclusion Robinson came to. Essentially, Robinson's philosophy was positive, even optimistic. He repeatedly made his position clear in letters to his friends and to others; moreover, it is implicit throughout his poetry.

Even before Latham posed his question, "What are we here for?", Robinson had been thinking about the meaning of life. As early as 1891 he wrote to Harry Smith:

Solitude . . . renders a man suspicious of the whole natural plan, and leads him to wonder whether the invisible powers are a fortuitous issue of unguided cosmos, or the cosmos itself. . . . Why have I not done differently? I cannot conscientiously say that it has been necessary that I should stay at home as I have; and the more I think it over, the more am I convinced that the fault lies with myself. But how about the unseen powers? The old buffers (no offence to them) will smoke their pipes and cut their coupons and tell us all about how the world is what we make it, and how every man is the architect of his own fortune, etc. It is good to hear them, but I sometimes have a clambering idea that perhaps there is another architect behind ourselves.

Robinson could not conceive of a maleficent deity, nor of a chaotic universe reeling through eons of endless time; to him the universe had both order and purpose, and man's transient life on earth was part of a larger plan. "The universe is a great thing, and the power of evil never put it together," he wrote Gledhill. "Of that I am certain and I am just as certain that this life is but one little scene in the big show." In 1894, commenting on the disparity between his own knowledge and Sir John Lubbock's "almost superhuman familiarity with the world's literature," Robinson wrote to Smith:

> . . . I cannot believe that these tremendous worldly differences are to be carried on through the second life. I cannot conceive of eternity as an endless panorama of "busted ambitions." That would be hell with a vengeance. I cannot believe that we poor devils deserve any such punishment. Life itself is no joke to a great percentage of us, and all things seem to point to an improvement of our condition when they are explained. I am not preaching, but I believe in immortality — I can't help it.

Gradually, as Robinson continued his spiritual quest, his convictions took the form of what is usually called philosophical idealism. Since philosophical idealism manifested itself in a variety of forms during the nineteenth century, it is more meaningful to define Robinson's idealism as modified transcendentalism, a composite of Carlyle, Emerson, and Swedenborg filtered through the mind and temperament of the poet. Robinson was a poet, not a philosopher, and in the poetry thought and expression are one in seamless art. Our purpose in distinguishing the major elements of his thought is to trace the development of his idealism in order to gain an understanding of his angle of vision.

In the spring of 1895 Robinson began a serious reading of the New Testament. If, as Neff states, it was the Scriptures' "value as literature" that struck Robinson initially, his reading was nonetheless an attempt to find out for himself what Christianity was essentially. Early in 1896 he met a Christian Scientist named Jones, a man who made a strong impression on Robinson. They discussed literature, religion and philosophy, questions of life and death, and the "triumph of mind over matter." At Jones's suggestion Robinson read Mary Baker Eddy's *Science and Health* and found himself "astonished and at times amused." About the same time Robinson reread Carlyle's *Sartor Resartus,* which had fascinated him as early as March 1891, at which time he was "completely soaked with its fiery philosophy," though there were many passages that he did not understand. Reading it again, in the fall of 1896, Robinson found that it not only made sense but that it also clarified much that hitherto had been obscure. He had, however, learned much in the past few years, and he had been moving in the direction of Carlyle's basic position for some time. He had become increasingly aware of the materialistic values of many who professed to be Christians, as well as of the misinterpretation and distortion of Christianity itself:

> As I am situated, I do not feel that I am in a place to make too much talk about anybody or anything; but it does make me positively sick to see the results of modern materialism as they are revealed in a town like this. I cannot joke over it as I used to; if I could, it would not affect me as it does. And when I add to this a vision of Trinity Church in Boston and a reflection of what it stands for, I begin to feel like breaking chairs, and wonder if a time is ever coming when the human race will acquire anything like a logical notion of human life — or, in other words, of Christianity.

He had found, too, that to live up to the ideals of Christianity was difficult. "I have been slowly getting rid of materialism for the past year or two," he wrote to Gledhill in October 1896, "but I fear I haven't the stamina to be a Christian — accepting Christ as either human or divine. Selfishness hangs to a man like a lobster and is the thing that keeps humanity where it is, I know that, but at present I am pretty much a human being, though I see a glimmer of the light once in a while and then meditate on possibilities." The position toward which Robinson had been moving was essentially Christian but without the dogmatism of any particular sect or creed. He had already rejected Calvinism and the orthodox conception of heaven and hell. In *Sartor Resartus* Robinson found expressed what he had been looking for. "If the book is anything," he wrote to Smith in November 1896, "it is a denial of the existence of matter as anything but a manifestation of thought. Christianity is the same thing, and so is illuminated commonsense. . . . Epictetus and Socrates, Emerson and Carlyle, Paul and Christ (or Jesus, if you prefer) tell pretty much the same story from a more general point of view." He did not believe in Christian Science, he said, "as anything apart from the spiritual wisdom that is latent in us all; but I do believe in idealism as the one logical and satisfactory interpretation of life. . . ."

Emerson also played a part in Robinson's transcendental idealism, probably more of a supporting role than a formative one. Although Robinson was acquainted with some of Emerson's work prior to the impact of *Sartor Resartus,* his early comments indicate neither enthusiasm nor an abiding interest. But in February 1897, having read what is perhaps Emerson's most transcendental essay, Robinson became very much excited: "I have just read Emerson on 'The Over-Soul.' If you do not know it, for heaven's sake get hold of it. In this I seem to find all that he was struggling to bring out in that eminently unsatisfactory essay on 'Compensation' — which is no more a measure of Emerson's genius than a cloudy dawn is of daylight." During the writing of "Captain Craig" Robinson again turned to Emerson, and his opinion of him remained high throughout his life. His esteem was not only for Emerson the essayist but also for Emerson the poet. More than once Robinson remarked that Emerson was America's greatest poet.

It would appear that Robinson's "conversion to idealism," to use Fussell's term, occurred in the fall of 1896, stimulated by his talks with Jones, clarified by his rereading of *Sartor Resartus,* and reinforced by his reading of Emerson's "The Over-Soul." The statement has often been made that the core of transcendentalism that runs through Robinson's poetry derives from his reading of Carlyle and Emerson. This is certainly true for the poems written during and after the fall of 1896. The "Octaves" in *The Children of the Night,* which were written in 1897, clearly stem from Robinson's recent enthusiastic encounter with Carlyle and Emerson. But an interesting question arises at this point: How to account for the transcendental note found in earlier poems? The manuscript of *The Torrent and The Night Before* was sent to the printer on September 12, 1896, and a number of poems included in that volume have transcendental overtones. "The Children of the Night," which is clearly "Emersonian," was published in January 1896; "Kosmos" goes back to some time before October 1895; "Supremacy" was begun as early as April 1892. And there are others. Because Robinson studied under Josiah Royce, one of the foremost proponents of philosophical idealism, some have attributed much of Robinson's thought to his influence. Though Robinson undoubtedly gained some acquaintance with the German idealists through Royce, it is doubtful that his course exerted much of an influence. Robinson's comments about Royce are all negative, and he frequently cut class. Moreover, systematic and abstract philosophic argument was not Robinson's forte; that is not the way his mind worked. As Mowry Saben once remarked to James L. Tryon, "The strength of Robinson was in his convictions, never in his opinions, which were veering as the wind. What he thought today he would unthink tomorrow, and this was true throughout his life. What he knew he knew intuitively, and not through any process of ratiocination. His convictions, however, were lasting and life-long." Saben's statement would suggest that Robinson came to Harvard with his deepest convictions already formed. If these convictions were somewhat "transcendental" or "idealistic" to begin with, even though Robinson may not have thought of them in those terms, it would account for much.

That such was the case is supported by a remark that Robinson made in a letter to his friend Chauncey Giles Hubbell, who was studying for the Swedenborgian ministry at the New-Church Theological School in Cambridge:

> Yes, I have lost my mother, but she is so much better off than she could possibly be here that it is no great strain on my idealism to put away my selfish sorrow for the change. There is a good deal of Swedenborg in my philosophy but Swedenborg is not enough. You will find the gist of it (as well as I can give it now) in the *Two Sonnets,* and in the last section of *Walt Whitman.*

The letter, dated 16 December, 1896, was written in reply to one from Hubbell expressing his pleasure over *The Torrent and The Night Before.* It is the reference to Swedenborg that is significant.

We are apt today to forget the seminal influence of Swedenborg's ideas throughout the past century. "No man can know the theology of the nineteenth century who has not read Swedenborg," said Henry Ward Beecher. "Swedenborgianism has done the liberating work of the last century. The statements of his religious works have revolutionized theology," remarked Edward Everett Hale. "The age is Swedenborg's," declared Emerson. Swedenborg repudiated the doctrines of original sin and predestination, the orthodox view of the Trinity, the idea of redemption through the atonement of Christ, and the belief that faith alone is sufficient for salvation. He thought that most Christian sects had misinterpreted Christianity in their doctrines and had misapplied it in practice. His concept of God was unitarian: God is One and in essence is Divine Love and Wisdom. Since He created the universe, all things partake of His essential nature; matter is a manifestation of Spirit. There are two worlds, a spiritual world and a natural world, and the natural world "corresponds" part for part to the spiritual world. Just as the sun of the natural world gives forth heat and light, so Divine Love and Divine Wisdom appear in the spiritual world as a sun that gives forth spiritual heat and light (love and wisdom). By means of divine influx this love and wisdom, the spirit of God, is accessible to man. Man has both reason and freedom of will; hence he can accept or reject the Divine Spirit. Love of self and love of the world, that is, sensual and material values, are a denial of spiritual values; they constitute a rejection of the Divine Spirit. Reliance on the inner spirit, man's higher self, is, as in Emerson, God-reliance. The ruling love of each person determines his spiritual condition; each person, in other words, creates his own heaven or hell, here and now as well as later. Knowledge of the good, however, is not sufficient for the good life; there is no such thing as faith without charity. According to Swedenborg's doctrine of use, everyone ought to use his life, his talents, for the benefit of others. In Swedenborgianism the ordinary concepts of time and space are meaningless. The spiritual world is eternally present, and though a constant struggle goes on between the internal and the external man, he should strive always to increase his degree of spirituality. Death is merely one more change of state toward complete spirituality.

The ideas of Swedenborg, coming as they did at a time of spiritual unrest, fell on fertile soil. Emerson, for example, although he rejected Swedenborg's specific and limited theological interpretation of nature, an interpretation, as he said, "that fastens each natural object to a theologic notion," had great respect for Swedenborg's bold genius, and thought that the doctrine of correspondence might possibly be a key "to unlock the meaning of the world." Whether this is true may be debatable, but it is one of the keys to unlock the meaning of Emerson. Swedenborg's concept of God as the creative principle radiating light or spirit through the uttermost reaches of the universe, the concept of influx, and the concept of nature, the physical world, as a veiled symbol — all these place Swedenborg in the developing line of Platonic and Neoplatonic thought that culminated in the philosophic idealism and transcendentalism of the nineteenth century.

Robinson's acquaintance with Swedenborgianism came through his association with the Swantons. The central figure in the story is Mrs. Swanton. When her son John Reed Swanton was asked whether Robinson would have become acquainted with the basic doctrines of Swedenborg through Mrs. Swanton, he replied, "You may be sure my mother would have repeatedly made clear her position and faith."

Mrs. Mary O. Swanton was a Swedenborgian from one of the leading Swedenborgian families in Maine. Her father served New-Church societies in Abington, Massachusetts and in Bath, Gardiner, and Portland, Maine. Her mother and her aunt were instrumental in organizing the Gardiner Society of the Church of the New Jerusalem in 1836. Her father-in-law was one of the founders of the Bath Society of the New Jerusalem. After the death of her husband in 1872, Mrs. Swanton lived in Gardiner with her three sons and her Aunt Dorcas. Their home was the heart of the Swedenborgian group in Gardiner; it was there that the weekly meetings of the Society were held. John Reed Swanton remembers that Dr. A. T. Schumann, Robinson's poetic mentor, "was a pretty regular attendant at a little parlor service my mother held on Sunday afternoons. . . ." This was at the time when Robinson and Dr. Schumann were working together on their poetry.[1]

Mrs. Swanton was active in the Maine Association of the New Jerusalem Church and in its educational activities. A delegate to the state meetings in the mid-eighties, she was appointed to a com-

---

[1] In the records of the Gardiner Society the entry for Dec. 7, 1884, lists Dr. Schumann among those in attendance. Though the doctor was not actually a member of the Society, there was a close connection between homeopathy and Swedenborgianism. Marguerite Block, in her study of *The New Church in the New World,* page 162, notes that "Homeopathy went like wild fire through the New Church. Its periodicals are full of discussions of its relation to the teachings of Swedenborg, and a large proportion of its membership embraced it."

mittee of seven "to establish reading circles in the State of Maine." In Gardiner, through her efforts, the discussion of Swedenborgianism was extended beyond the members of the Society; she was instrumental in setting up and maintaining a series of public meetings over a period of two months each summer for several years. The purpose of these meetings was educational. Leaders of national prominence in the Swedenborgian movement presented a series of lectures which constituted a course in the doctrines of Emanuel Swedenborg. "These meetings," Mrs. Swanton noted at the end of the summer of 1885, "have given great satisfaction and been well attended." The average attendance for morning meetings was eighty to one hundred; for the evening, one hundred to one hundred and fifty. In a small town of approximately 5,500 inhabitants, such an attendance reflects no small degree of interest. That the rector of the Episcopal church, as a result of these meetings, should have devoted a sermon to a blasting denunciation of the doctrines of Swedenborg is evidence of a lively controversy in the community.

In the teachings of Swedenborg, said John Reed Swanton, "Love is primary; intention counts but not mere lip service or profession of faith." Utterly selfless, Mrs. Swanton devoted her life to her family, her friends, and her church. According to an article that appeared in *The New-Church Messenger* after her death in 1923, "She was not merely a believer in the Doctrines; they were her constant thought, the accompaniment of every breath she drew." An exemplar of what she believed and taught, "She made her home one in which her boys loved to be, . . . it came to be the gathering place for a considerable band. . . . and not a few attributed their later success and happiness to her influence. One frequently numbered among these was Edward [*sic*] Arlington Robinson, the poet." Robinson's early transcendentalism was grounded in the teachings of Swedenborg.

This does not mean that Robinson was a Swedenborgian. He said himself that "Swedenborg is not enough." But it does account for the transcendental note in some of the early poems and helps to explain them. It also makes clear that Robinson's adoption of idealism as the "one logical and satisfactory interpretation of life" was not a "conversion" but hard-won intellectual clarification and confirmation of convictions he had already formed but which now rested on a broader and firmer base.

Though Robinson's thought has an affinity with that of the earlier transcendentalists, it is not identical with theirs. There is little of the typical transcendental attitude toward nature, the third member, with God and man, of the transcendental trinity. Nor is there much of the buoyant exuberance of Emerson or Whitman. In some respects Robinson is closer to Hawthorne and Melville. He knew from personal experience and observation the painful limitations of human life, the tortured complexity of the human psyche, the essential loneliness of each individual, the estrangement of man from man, from himself, and from God. Yet he referred to himself as a "transcendental optimist." In April 1897 he tried to explain to Smith what he meant: "There's a good deal to live for, but a man has to go through hell really to find it out. The process is hard but the result pays. If it didn't there would be no universe. This may sound obscure, but it isn't." And a few weeks later, he added the statement: "This world is a grind and the sooner we make up our minds to the fact the better it will be for us. That, to my mind, is the real optimism." Whereas the naturalist would say, "Life is hell; therefore it has no meaning," Robinson said in effect, "Life is hell; therefore it does have meaning." The difference is enormous. Robinson could not accept a mechanistic-materialistic view of the universe. He accepted the inevitable limitations of human existence, but he did not think that all of life's difficulties were inevitable. He was aware of the disintegrating forces at work in contemporary society — indeed, he was appalled by them — and he saw that these forces stemmed from a materialistic philosophy that made of life a cycle of self-perpetuating futility. This is one of the major themes in Robinson's work, and his philosophy is the measure of value against which the lives of others, including the characters in his poems, are weighed. Long before Eliot's "The Waste Land" and Auden's "The Age of Anxiety," Robinson mirrored the spiritual sterility of an age that was to hurl itself into two world wars and go crashing along on a "blind atomic pilgrimage." As early as March 1897, meditating on the difference between his own views and the materialistic tendencies of the age, Robinson wrote Smith with scathing sarcasm:

. . . how the devil is a man to understand things in an age like this, when the whole trend of popular thought is in the wrong direction — not only that, but proud of the way it is taking? The age is all right, material progress is all right, Herbert Spencer is all right, hell is all right. These things are temporal necessities, but they are damned uninteresting to one who can get a glimpse of the real light through the clouds of time. It is that glimpse that makes me wish to live and see it out. . . . The great scholars of the world are for the most part spiritual imbeciles, and there is where the trouble lies. The willingness "to be a child again" comes hard — so hard that it will never come to many who are in the world today. That is not what they are here for. "The world was made in order, and the atoms march in time." It is a damned queer time to us who are here now; but it is all right and we are all going to hear it as it is — when the mortal wax gets out of our ears.

It was with courage and a realization of the hardship involved that Robinson went ahead with his chosen task, not at all certain about the immediate future, but secure in the knowledge that he had a "place in the scheme of things."

At the same time that Robinson was clarifying his philosophical views, he was sharpening his literary perceptions. Although he never made an extended, systematic statement of his literary principles, we can piece together from various sources his basic ideas about literature in general and poetry in particular. Of special interest are the ideas he expressed during the period 1893–1897, culminating in the publication of *The Children of the Night,* for it was during that time that he began to see rather clearly the direction his poetry should take. Oddly enough, we can gain a better understanding both of his literary concepts and of his poetry if we start with the topic of fiction.

After his two years at Harvard, Robinson returned to Gardiner with the avowed intention of becoming a writer. "This itch for authorship," he wrote Gledhill in October 1893, "is worse than the devil and about spoils a man for anything else." A short time later, in a letter to Smith, Robinson referred to himself as a "literary man" and spoke of a career in "literature." It is notable that Robinson at this time was thinking of himself as author in a more inclusive sense than poet. He gave himself two or three years to prove himself. His head full of ideas, he fixed up his room as a study and began to write — "sketches" (Robinson disliked calling them short stories, though he sometimes referred to them as prose tales), his collaborative metrical translation of *Antigone,* and, from time to time, poems. From the outset he had hopes of publishing the translation — hopes, by the way, which never materialized. Three of his poems were published in the fall of 1894, but it was not until the fall of 1895 that he began to think seriously of putting together a volume of poems. His major efforts throughout 1894 and 1895 were devoted to his sketches, though he found it increasingly difficult to resist the lure of poetry. During this period he wrote approximately fifteen sketches for a projected volume of 350 to 400 pages to be entitled *Scattered Lives.*[1] "Some day," he wrote Smith in April 1895, "you will see a printed edition of *Scattered Lives* even though it be printed on toilet paper with a one-hand printing press." Clearly Robinson intended to make his entry into the literary world as a writer of prose fiction.

What is one to make of this shift of emphasis from what hitherto had been Robinson's absorbing interest and driving force? To say, as some have said, that his venture into prose fiction was a temporary diversion is only superficially true. The fact is that Robinson's interest in fiction bore a significant relationship to his poetry.

Two things Robinson needed at this time: enough money to pay his way, and some measure of success to satisfy his sense of personal worth and to justify himself in the eyes of his townspeople. His agonizing sense of financial dependence and his even greater fear of failure run like a double theme through the letters of this period. The obvious reason for Robinson's turning to prose was that the market was larger and more profitable than the market for poetry. But the real reason lies deeper and stems from Robinson's literary values. Robinson had no intention of becoming a hack journalist writing potboilers to satisfy the popular taste. When he began work on his sketches, he made an initial assessment of himself and the situation:

. . . I think I have a little originality, but have I the genius for selection that is the one requisite of a literary man next to an easy flow of

---

[1] Sutcliffe misread the title as *Scattered Lines.*

language? — Not necessarily rapid, but easy in effect. I could never make a rapid writer; I am too fussy. I have fiddled too much over sonnets and ballades. I demand a certain something in the arrangement of words, and more in their selection, that I find in very few of our writers today. The question is — will it be found in what I write? and if it is, will the public care anything about it? I do not wholly believe in art for art's sake, but I do not think that anything is good literature when art is wholly sacrificed to the subject matter.

Much as he wanted acceptance of his work, he must first satisfy himself. Success must be achieved on his own terms, and his standards were high.

Whatever else was requisite to good literature, it must be a work of art. With a critical eye, Robinson turned his attention to the study of prose fiction. Much of his reading was in contemporary fiction. He measured American, British, and French performance, and compared contemporary work with that of the past. He was especially impressed by the French writers, whose works he read in the original. He noted that both Cherbuliez and Daudet were gifted "with an extensive vocabulary of common words for describing common things." Reading Daudet's *Tartarin de Tarascon,* Robinson said he did not at first understand how a man was able to write such a book, but then he concluded that "he did it by hard work. . . . the author makes every sentence count." After reading Hall Caine's *The Manxman,* competing with DuMaurier's sensational *Trilby* as the bestseller of the year, Robinson thought that Caine proved "his greatness by making the book a success in spite of its fearful length." But he noted too that "Scene after scene is spoiled by over preparation and half the book is worse than padding." It was, however, superior to *Trilby,* in which "The 'story' comes in and spoils it all." The idea of comparing DuMaurier with Thackeray seemed to Robinson "utterly ridiculous." The contrast between Caine's work and Hawthorne's *The Blithedale Romance* he found "bewildering." "How did Hawthorne do it?" he asked. Again he concluded that Hawthorne "was capable of an amount of brain racking and tinkering of which the modern ink-spiller has no conception." He was disappointed with Kipling's *Many Inventions* because "There was too much journalistic stuffing in it." In his own work, Robinson became aware of his "artistic deficiencies." He noted "a pestering tendency to repeat small expressions" and his "old fault of overcondensation." Constantly dissatisfied, he wrote and rewrote his sketches with painstaking care, experimenting in various ways in "aching earnest in the cause of art and strength," until finally on March 3, 1895, he could write to Smith with an inner radiance: "I think it is the knowledge (or at least the belief) that I can do anything, in my own way, that I undertake."

Art, in the narrow sense of craftsmanship, Robinson knew was only one side of the literary coin. The ultimate value of literature depended equally on what the author had to say. And some things were more important than others. Robinson praised Cherbuliez because his work was "so true to life that he startles one at times"; he read *L'Idée de Jean Têterol* twice and "felt a broadening of my humanity after each reading." Of one of François Coppée's stories of the humble and afflicted, he remarked, "One of the most human things ever written." Shakespeare, Robinson's favorite writer, was a constant inspiration; *Measure for Measure* left him "thunderstruck." "Dark as the subject is," he wrote, "there is a rich vein of a rather broad humor running through the play which lends to the whole thing that wonderfully human effect which is a synonym for Shakspere." Daudet's *Jack,* which Henry James called "a brilliant photography of pain," as Robinson noted, impressed him as "a great book . . . and ought to do its work in the world in the way of opening people's eyes and widening their sympathies." Hardy, whose works he had been reading since 1891, he thought would "be great after Caine is totally forgotten." He never "fully realized the greatness of Hawthorne" until he read *The Marble Faun:* "There is a sense of reality about it which is utterly wanting in *The Scarlet Letter;* and there is a kind of glorification of little things which only a great master is likely to find worth while." After reading J. H. Rosny's *L'Impérieuse Bonté,* Robinson was not sure that it was a great novel but he was certain that it was a great book: "It deals with the dark puzzles of life in a way that must make a man think, but it is never fanatical or illogical. . . . The universality of the book is astonishing, and we feel and see the hand that moves the world, '*la main que pousse le monde,*' as we read it." When Rudyard Kipling wrote an animal story entitled "Kaa's Hunting," Robinson did not care for it; he preferred "Mulvaney and his comrades to snakes and monkeys. . . . I prefer men and women who live, breathe, talk, fight, make love, or go to the devil after the

manner of human beings. Art is only valuable to me when it reflects humanity or at least human emotions."

In his prose sketches Robinson was attempting to say something,
in artistic form, about the human condition, something that all
great writers, whether in prose or in poetry, have tried to do. Robinson later destroyed the manuscripts of these sketches, but we
have a record of most of the titles and themes. As a group they are
highly revealing. One, untitled, dealt "with the selfishness of self-
denial — a peculiar but by no means rare flaw of human nature";
"Anxious Hendricks" was a "sketch of a philosophical tramp . . .
looking for a rest"; "Parable of the Pines" was concerned with "the
philosophical enmity of two brothers who were not born for the
same purpose"; "The Black Path" was "a little study in darkness";
"Lachesis" was "a marionette story touching lightly on divorce";
"Christmas Eve," later entitled "The Ruins of Bohemia," reflected
the "wasted part of a brilliant but 'unruddered' man in the company of a poor devil he has taken as a companion for the simple
reason that he can master him"; "Saturday," later entitled "Al-
cander," was "founded on the amiable portrait of one Mr. Hutchings in bed with a pint of rum and a pile of dime novels." These
sketches were studies of character and personal relationships drawn
from a philosophical and psychological point of view. Conflicting
philosophical values, psychological kinks — "scattered lives" indeed! Though one or two of the sketches seem to have been somewhat fanciful, it is clear that Robinson was turning to the lives of
those around him for material. And he did so consciously and
deliberately. When Harry de Forest Smith remarked on Robinson's perceptive powers, his ability to see even "the wrinkles on the
cerebrum of the men and women" he met, Robinson replied:
"There is more in every person's soul than we think. Even the
happy mortals we term ordinary or commonplace act their own
mental tragedies and live a far deeper and wider life than we are
inclined to believe possible in the light of our prejudices." In an
introspective and self-critical vein, Robinson continued:

> . . . I must acknowledge the dismal truth that the majority of man-
> kind interest me only as studies. They are to me "a little queer," like
> the Quaker's wife. . . . I tread a narrow path, in one sense, but I do
> a considerable amount of observing. In fact, I observe so much that

my feet often slip and I am forever stumbling over little things that other men never notice. This is one of my drawbacks, but it is not without its benefits; it opens one's eyes to the question of happiness and leads him to analyse that mysterious element of human nature from many points of view.

Like Henry James, Robinson had taken on the role of observer, less concerned with transferring his own personal emotions to the page than he was with representing objectively the thoughts and feelings of people in various situations.

Given Robinson's interest in the motive forces of human behavior, it is not surprising that he should have turned to prose fiction at this time. His subject matter called for narrative treatment. Moreover, the boom in the fiction market was the result of an increasing demand that literature concern itself with life. In France, England, and in the United States, "realism" was the dynamic mode and fiction the dynamic vehicle. Though there were arguments as to just how "fidelity to life" was to be achieved, the movement as a whole was toward greater freedom of expression and a widening of the bounds of subject matter. But as fiction moved closer to reality, poetry moved farther away into the genteel and vaporous dreamland described in Chapter 1. The important and exciting point here is that Robinson was moving in the same general direction as fiction — not only in his sketches but also in his poetry. As early as October 1893 he had written Smith, "There is poetry in all types of humanity — even in lawyers and horse-jockeys — if we are willing to search it out. . . ." It was in May 1894, in the midst of his prose writing, that he wrote his plea for a poet "To put these little sonnet-men to flight." At the same time he began "a tragic monologue" entitled "The Night Before," which was to occupy the climactic position in Robinson's first volume.[1] A longish poem of nearly four hundred lines, "The Night Before" is a rather melodramatic story of mental anguish, of betrayed love and murderous hate. "The main purpose of the thing," Robinson commented, "is to show that men and women are individuals; and there is a minor injunction running through it not to thump a man too hard when he is down. . . . I write it because

[1] C. P. Smith reports a "lost first draft" begun on the night of Herman and Emma's wedding.

I cannot help it, and this is also true of the way in which I do it."
Originally cast in unrhymed tetrameters, it was changed to blank
verse as Robinson revised it for publication. Not one of his better
poems, and excluded from the *Collected Poems,* it was nonetheless
an important step in the poet's work, for it marked his first poetic
attempt to deal with character portrayal and to write a long narrative poem. Moreover, it was closely related to his work in prose.
At one point in the poem the narrator remarks:

> The woes I suffered
> After that hard betrayal made me
> Pity, at first, all breathing creatures
> On this bewildered earth. I studied
> Their faces and made for myself the story
> Of all their scattered lives.

In a very real sense "The Night Before" is another of Robinson's
sketches; he had merely shifted from narrative prose to narrative
poetry. Robinson's writing of prose fiction was not a divergence
from his main work, for it contributed to the development of his
poetic maturity. The prose sketches were an outgrowth of his basic
interest in people, and his poetic character sketches and longer
narrative poems were, at least in part, an outgrowth of his work in
prose. He was moving in the direction of Tilbury Town and his
own personal idiom. The prose sketches are gone, but *Scattered
Lives* was published nonetheless, not as prose but as poetry. Robinson's concern for the "mortals we term ordinary or commonplace"
was ever central, and the record of their "scattered lives" is the
heart of his life work. As he said in "Calverly's,"

> No fame delays oblivion
> For them, but something yet survives:
> A record written fair, could we
> But read the book of scattered lives.

When a poet writes a poem decrying the barren state of poetry
and calling for a poet to give it life, one can be sure that the poet
has already nominated his candidate for the job. But such a charge
puts the poet under an obligation to do more than criticize. If the
poet is merely a disgruntled poetaster, the plaint will be recognized

for the whimper that it is when nothing more is forthcoming. If the poet is a serious artist, one can expect the poet to come forth with corrective measures in the form of poems. That Robinson was dissatisfied with much of contemporary verse, there is ample evidence. In "Oh for a poet" he attributed the poetic blight not to the times but to poets who though technically proficient produce lifeless and insignificant verse. And he offered his remedy: the way to revive poetry was to bring it back to life, to close the gap between poetry and reality. It is clear that "Oh for a poet" was a turning point in Robinson's work and that the program of action called for was partly the result of Robinson's interest in and awareness of what was going on in fiction. But fiction was not the whole story; poetry also played a part in shaping his ideas and giving direction to his own poetry. Except by negative example, it was not contemporary poetry but poetry of the past that was influential, especially the work of Cowper and of Crabbe. Robinson's reading of Cowper was particularly significant and immediately preceded the writing of "Oh for a poet."

Robinson's French lessons were over in April 1894. On May 5 he sent the manuscripts of three prose sketches to the *Atlantic Monthly* but with little hope that they would be accepted. In mid-April, at the time when his love affair was breaking up, he had begun reading William Cowper's long blank-verse poem, *The Task*. Was there a sense of identity with this gentle soul of the late eighteenth century, also disappointed in love, who wrote poetry to stave off bouts of melancholia? Be that as it may, Robinson was soon writing to Smith of his enthusiasm for Cowper. Although he thought Cowper's religion "akin to mawkish," he nonetheless was drawn to him:

> He was a strange man; and this strangeness, with his almost pathetic sincerity, go to make up the reason for my fondness for his poetry. He stands between Thomson and Wordsworth, and for some reason, he seems to stand on pretty firm ground. I do not think another half-century will disturb him to any great extent. His description of the wood-cutter and his dog cannot die while men and women care for true art in homely things.

In addition to reading *The Task,* Robinson also read the selections from Cowper's works included in Thomas Humphry Ward's *The*

English Poets. He apparently also read Ward's introductory essay on Cowper, for Robinson's remarks to Smith echo Ward's at a number of points. Included in this volume is a selection from *Table Talk,* editorially entitled "The Past and Future of Poetry," in which Cowper traces the decline of poetry from the time of Eden down through the time of Pope, who "Made poetry a mere mechanic art," to his own time in which "servile trick and imitative knack / Confine the million in the beaten track." Cowper sees a remedy only in the return of poetry to universal sources; in effect he calls for a poet-beacon, a poet whose verse will "shed illuminating rays / On every scene and subject it surveys." In the margin, Robinson, who rarely marked his books, set off the passage immediately following and drew a line beside these verses:

> And 'tis the sad complaint, and almost true,
> Whate'er we write, we bring forth nothing new.
> 'Twere new indeed to see a bard all fire,
> Touched with a coal from heaven, assume the lyre,
> And tell the world, still kindling as he sung,
> With more than mortal music on his tongue,
> That He who died below, and reigns above,
> Inspires the song, and that his name is Love.

Robinson's call for a poet was precipitated by one of the forerunners of romanticism; his initial response was made in terms of contemporary realism, though his full response would be more inclusive. This conjunction of romanticism and realism is not so strange as it seems, for despite the tendency to regard the two as polar opposites, they are not incompatible; indeed, they share some common ground. The romantic revival, in its reaction against the artificiality and sterility of an exhausted neoclassicism, manifested itself in a return to the natural. Romanticism, whatever other characteristics it developed, had a realistic base. Cowper was, as Ward accurately perceived, "the beginning of a new order in poetry." The parallel between the poetic situation at the end of the eighteenth century and the end of the nineteenth century is too obvious to need comment, and it surely did not escape Robinson. We must not, however, jump to the unwarranted conclusion that Robinson is to be identified solely with the realistic tradition. His realism was a large part of his strength, but he also had strong ties to other poets and aspects of the romantic tradition and to the classical tradition as well. He was classical in his restraint and sense of form, romantic in his idealism and range, and realistic in his honesty and objectivity. In time these components would fuse into a harmonious relationship and result in a style that was Robinson's own, a sensitive reflector of the texture of his mind and personality. At the moment he was adding a realistic dimension.

In early June, Robinson's sketches were returned from the *Atlantic Monthly,* "damned rather pleasantly" just as he had predicted. Despite the rejection, he continued with his prose work, but when, a week later, *The Critic* accepted "Oh for a poet," the turn toward poetry had been started. W. H. Thorne, editor of *The Globe,* unwittingly helped complete the turn. Thorne was a friend of Caroline Davenport Swan and visited at her home in the summer of 1894. The September *Globe* was dominated by the work of the Gardiner group: two essays by Miss Swan, a poem by Henry S. Webster, two poems by Dr. Schumann, and two poems, "The House on the Hill" and "The Miracle," by E. A. Robinson. In an editorial postscript to an article criticizing contemporary New England writers, Thorne singled out the Gardiner writers as exceptions, evidence that "there is still a good deal of literary genius in New England." He gave a word of praise to each. "Mr. Robinson," he remarked, "bids fair to outshine all competitors in his native state." This was the first public acknowledgment of Robinson's poetry.

Encouraged, Robinson increased his poetic output, gradually at first, then more swiftly. One by one he sent his poems off to the journals — *The Dial, The Century, Chap-Book, Lippincott's Magazine, The Cosmopolitan, Youth's Companion* — and one by one most of them were returned. In February 1895 he was overjoyed when *Lippincott's* sent him a check for seven dollars for his sonnet "For a Copy of Poe's Poems," which he had previously sent to *The Dial.* It was his first "blood-money." "A check tomorrow for a thousand would not give me the same sensation," he wrote. That the sonnet would not be published for eleven years, he had of course no way of knowing. By March he found it increasingly hard to continue working on his prose sketches. "My worst and

most persistent enemy . . . is a constant inclination to write poetry,"
he wrote to Smith. "Sometimes I am half afraid the damned stuff
will kill what little ability I have." By November, with one more
poem published in *The Globe* and another about to be printed in
The Critic, he had yielded; he was "making all sorts of poems."
Aware that most editors were indifferent, if not hostile, toward his
poems, he resolved to try the book publishers. He stringently revised his early poems, added his recent ones, and in late February
or early March 1896 sent them out under the title *The Tavern and
The Night Before.* His first venture "proved a fizzle." So did the
second. Desperate for a hearing, he decided to print the volume at
his own expense. He cut it from a hundred pages to forty-four and
changed the title. The Riverside Press would do the job for fifty-
two dollars. Early in December the book arrived — 312 copies of
a blue paper-covered pamphlet entitled *The Torrent and The Night
Before.* On December 4, 1896, Robinson began sending out in-
scribed copies to editors, critics, professors, novelists, and poets,
and to his friends. By December 22 all the copies had been dis-
tributed. The course of his life hung in the balance.

He had his own opinions of the purpose and worth of his work.
At the time when his manuscript was first rejected, he wrote to
Harry Smith:

> I have done a few things which I know are worth while and that is
> a great deal to be sure of. If printed lines are good for anything,
> they are bound to be picked up some time; and then, if some poor
> devil of a man or woman feels any better or any stronger for any-
> thing that I have said, I shall have no fault to find with the scheme
> or anything in it. I am inclined to be a trifle solemn in my verses,
> but I intend that there shall always be at least a suggestion of some-
> thing wiser than hatred and something better than despair.

Announcing his forthcoming volume to his friend Arthur Gledhill,
Robinson clearly indicated his own awareness of the difference
between his work and the conventional poetry of the period:

> You won't find much in the way of natural description. There is
> very little tinkling water, and there is not a red-bellied robin in the
> whole collection. When it comes to "nightingales and roses" I am
> not "in it" nor have I the smallest desire to be. I sing, in my own

particular manner, of heaven & hell and now and then of natural things (supposing they exist) of a more prosy connotation than those generally admitted into the domain of metre. In short I write whatever I think is appropriate to the subject and let tradition go to the deuce.

To Edith Brower, a writer who quickly became one of Robinson's most devoted admirers and with whom he carried on an extensive correspondence for many years, he wrote in words whose humor is lost in sharpness, "You may consider the whole thing as a kind of self-defence against the abject materialism of a 'down east' community whereof the whole purpose of life is 'to get a job' and to vote a straight Republican ticket."[1]

The critical response to *The Torrent and The Night Before* was generally favorable, sufficient to confirm Robinson's judgment of his own powers. Most of the response came in the form of personal letters of acknowledgment, though at least eighteen notices or reviews of the book appeared in various journals and newspapers across the country. Of the reviews, Harry Thurston Peck's in *The Bookman* has achieved a dubious kind of fame, not because its judgment was accurate but because it elicited Robinson's trenchant response to the charge of pessimism. Although Peck praised Robinson for the "true fire in his verse" and "the swing and singing of wind and wave and the passion of human-emotion in his lines," he thought the poet's limitations "vital": "His humor is of a grim sort and the world is not beautiful to him, but a prison-house." To which Robinson replied, "I am sorry to learn that I have painted myself in such lugubrious colours. The world is not a 'prison-house,' but a kind of spiritual kindergarten, where millions of bewildered infants are trying to spell God with the wrong blocks." The negative criticism of Peck and a few others was more than offset by words of praise from such men as Barrett Wendell, J. J. Hays, Charles Eliot Norton, and Dean Briggs, all of Harvard. Horace Scudder, the editor of the *Atlantic Monthly* who had previously rejected Robinson's sketches, expressed his "pleasure at

---

[1] Robinson's letters to Miss Brower are now in the Colby College Library. I am indebted to Mrs. William Nivison and to Professor Cary for permission to cite from the manuscripts.

poetry which has so much warm blood in its veins." Edward Eggleston, noted for his realistic treatment of the Indiana backwoods country, wrote Robinson enthusiastically ("Let a total stranger hail you with admiration . . ."), and in an interview in *The Outlook* praised Robinson for his originality and for sending him "a book that I cannot help reading." Nathan H. Dole, translator of Tolstoy and Daudet, reviewed the book and found the poems "vital, virile expressions of a wholly modern spirit" and expressed the hope that Robinson would continue "in the same free, bold course." Robinson was satisfied; he had found out what he wanted to know. Now he had to get his poems before the public.

One happy consequence of *The Torrent and The Night Before* was Robinson's friendship with the Henry Richards family. A cultured and civic-minded family, the Richardses played an important part in local affairs. They also played an important part in Robinson's life. Laura E. Richards, herself a writer of children's stories and verses, offered understanding and support throughout the years. Henry Richards, the eldest son, later a teacher at Groton School, was indirectly responsible for what became a major turning point in Robinson's career. Through the Richards family, Robinson also met John Hays Gardiner, then assistant professor of English at Harvard, whose early appreciation and encouragement of Robinson's work meant much to the young poet. In the year following his mother's death, Robinson's close association with the Richards family made his last year in Gardiner bearable and at times even pleasurable. Nonetheless, for personal and professional reasons, he felt the need to get away.

By fall Robinson had made arrangements with a Boston firm to publish his work, the cost to be borne by the author. William Butler, a Boston friend, contributed the money. Robinson deleted two poems from *The Torrent and The Night Before,* added sixteen, including a group of twenty-five octaves, and called the new volume *The Children of the Night.* A quarrel with Herman in November 1897 resulted in Robinson's leaving the household. By December, when the book came out, he had left Gardiner and was living in New York.

For practical purposes *The Torrent and The Night Before* and *The Children of the Night* can be regarded as one book. And what a remarkable book it is! From the time of its publication in 1897 until Robert Frost's *A Boy's Will* in 1913, there is not a single volume of American poetry to compare with it except the next two volumes of Robinson's own work. Most first books of poetry are later sources of embarrassment to their authors; the work too often fails because the vehicle is inadequate to the thought or because the technique is so overriding that matter is subordinated to manner. There is relatively little of such weakness in *The Children of the Night,* and what little there was, Robinson excluded from the *Collected Poems.* What strikes one, even in the light of Robinson's later development, is the maturity of the work as a whole, the range of thought and feeling and the expressiveness of the medium.

The poems can be divided into three large, though somewhat overlapping, categories: poems about literature and authors, character sketches and narratives, and poems of a more general nature that are primarily reflective or philosophic. In the first group, in addition to "Dear Friends" and "Oh for a poet," are several that deal with the nature and function of a poet. The sonnet beginning "The master and the slave go hand in hand" presents the paradoxical relationship of the poet to his art: only in the poet-slave's understanding of "The mission of his bondage" to his master, art, can the poet through the magic of words become the master of his art, a feat which, especially in a sonnet, can seldom if ever be completely achieved. "Octave I" clearly states Robinson's poetic credo:

> To get at the eternal strength of things,
> And fearlessly to make strong songs of it,
> Is, to my mind, the mission of that man
> The world would call a poet. He may sing
> But roughly, and withal ungraciously;
> But if he touch to life the one right chord
> Wherein God's music slumbers, and awake
> To truth one drowsed ambition, he sings well.

This octave was not included in the *Collected Poems,* possibly because Robinson then felt, especially after some of the excesses of the free-verse movement and also because of the direction his own poetry had taken, that strength could be attained without singing "roughly" and "ungraciously;" but its presence in the original *The*

Children of the Night is an important index to the intensity of his feelings at a time when the prevalent practice was to sing sweetly and prettily. "Octave XXI" (XIX in the *Collected Poems*) expresses much the same idea in words that strongly echo Emerson's poet of strength, "Merlin." Seven poems, six of them sonnets, are concerned with individual authors — Zola, Matthew Arnold, George Crabbe, Thomas Hood, Thomas Hardy, Verlaine, and Walt Whitman, a singular and motley collection. Of the group, only Matthew Arnold was held in any esteem; Crabbe and Hood were minor figures, scarcely read; the other four were highly controversial, more notorious than famous. Yet for Robinson they shared in the enduring quality of art that is basically human and true; moreover, their achievement, though generally unappreciated, was a commentary on the pettiness of the present. Crabbe, for example, whose "hard, human pulse is throbbing still / With the sure strength that fearless truth endows," pointed up

> the shame
> And emptiness of what our souls reveal
> In books that are as altars where we kneel
> To consecrate the flicker, not the flame.

As for Whitman,

> We do not hear him very much to-day:
> His piercing and eternal cadence rings
> Too pure for us — too powerfully pure,
> Too lovingly triumphant, and too large;
> But there are some that hear him, and they know
> That he shall sing to-morrow for all men,
> And that all time shall listen.

Appropriately, Robinson used for "Walt Whitman" not the sonnet but a freer form made up of three blank-verse stanzas of varying lengths with a short last line.

Tilbury Town is as closely associated with E. A. Robinson as Yoknapatawpha County is with William Faulkner. Like Faulkner, indeed like all great writers, Robinson created his own world out of his own observation and vision. To the reader this world is revealed as gradually as it was built, for it was shaped poem by

poem and it grew with the poet's growing acquaintance and understanding of it. To see Tilbury Town only as Gardiner, Maine, is a
partial view, though the fictitious map of Tilbury squares with
Gardiner pretty well. To see it as a small New England town
places it in better perspective, but it is still a limited view; for
Tilbury Town is a world of people, not of places, and the essentially human is not dependent on place or time. In the character
sketches and brief narrative poems in *The Children of the Night*
Robinson began to people Tilbury Town, and it is there that we
first meet its inhabitants: the miser, Aaron Stark, with "eyes like
little dollars in the dark"; the bereaved and tormented lover, Luke
Havergal, with "the fiery night" in his eyes; "the skirt-crazed repro-
bate," John Evereldown, who follows "the women wherever they
call"; the wealthy and envied gentleman, Richard Cory, who "Went
home and put a bullet through his head"; the wry but happy Cliff
Klingenhagen, who "took the draught / Of bitterness himself"; the
butcher, Reuben Bright, who "cried like a great baby half that
night." There are others, unnamed, whose stories are told in "Her
Eyes," "The Story of the Ashes and the Flame," and "The Pity of
the Leaves." These are the first of what would become a gallery of
portraits, not lush with color, but chiaroscuros, vignettes of light
and shade, or incisive delineations in dry point. Later would come
Captain Craig, Isaac and Archibald, Miniver Cheevy, Flammonde,
Old King Cole, Pamela, Llewellyn, Mr. Flood, Avenel Gray, and
others. The names of Robinson's characters are frequently unusual, either to symbolize the character or to achieve particulariza-
tion without any possibility of identification with actual people; in
either case, they help to give a sense of universality to the characters. Even the name of Tilbury Town is symbolic. Hagedorn
suggests that it stands for "a cash-box, a till, this modern age in
miniature"; Neff identifies it with "the tilbury, a smart two-wheeled
open carriage of those days." Though Robinson would have appreciated Hagedorn's pun, Neff's reference is more likely, though
he doesn't make clear why Tilbury is an appropriate name. Both
the name and its connotation may have been suggested by a scene
in Robinson's favorite novel, *Pendennis*. In Chapter 36, "Where
Pen Appears in Town and Country," Major Pendennis, pompous
and worldy-wise, attempts to teach his nephew Arthur, a budding

poet, how to get ahead in a vain society where money and position are all-important; bursting with self-importance because of his nodding acquaintance with titled and wealthy people, he tells his nephew, "yes, depend on it, my boy; for a poor man, there is nothing like having good acquaintances." He draws Arthur's attention to a "dark blue brougham" belonging to Sir Hugh Trumpington, who "was never known to walk in his life." Then to indicate his own high station, the Major says proudly, "Well, that brougham is mine if I choose, between four and seven. Just as much mine as if I jobbed it from Tilbury's, begad, for thirty pound a-month." The Tilbury, then, was a status symbol, much the same as a Cadillac is for some people today.

It is primarily in the reflective and philosophic poems of *The Children of the Night* that Robinson's characteristic themes and imagery begin to emerge. The transience of life and the inevitability of change and death are expressed in such poems as "The House on the Hill" (originally subtitled "Villanelle of Departure"), "Villanelle of Change," "The Chorus of Old Men in 'Aegeus,' " "Three Quatrains," and "The Clerks." Though the theme is essentially the same, these poems vary considerably in form and treatment. As a group they illustrate Robinsons versatile command of form and his flexible control of language and tone.

The villanelle, exemplified by the first two of these poems, is one of those old French forms on which Robinson cut his metrical eye-teeth, and for which he confessed a kind of fascination, though he was aware of their limitations. Highly artificial in form, the villanelle is generally considered to be appropriate for the expression of grace and charm; in the late nineteenth century it was frequently used for light verse of a humorous or trivial nature. Robinson's use of the villanelle for a serious subject was unconventional but not inappropriate, for the repetitiveness of the form itself, the cyclical rhyme and refrain, and the muted tone both help to reinforce the theme.

"The Chorus of Old Men in 'Aegeus,' " an outgrowth of Robinson's work on *Antigone* and his interest in Greek drama, is not a translation but an attempt to capture the Greek spirit in a choral ode such as Sophocles might have written in his lost play about Aegeus. The poem is based on the story of Aegeus, King of Athens, whose son Theseus had sailed away to Crete, pledged to deliver Athens from the scourge of the Minotaur. The signal of success was to be white sails in place of the usual black ones. On his return, however, Theseus neglected to change the sails; Aegeus, thinking his son dead, killed himself. At this point in the imaginary play, Robinson has the old men of the city utter their choral commentary of grief and tragic acceptance. Composed of two sets of perfectly symmetrical stanzas, the poem is a marvel of parallelism and balance, not only of form but of thought and feeling. The first two stanzas, in which the old men pray to the gods to

> Look with a just regard,
> And with an even grace,
> Here on the shattered corpse of a shattered king,

and to

> Receive him once again
> Who now no longer moves
> Here in this flickering dance of changing days,

are made up of twelve unrhymed lines each, a series of alternating pentameter and trimeter lines arranged in the pattern 555 33 555 3333. The last two stanzas, in which the old men utter their lament and final acceptance, are made up of ten lines each, in which hexameter lines (twice the length of a trimeter) alternate in the first four lines with pentameters and succeed the trimeter lines in the pattern 6565 336 336; these hexameters not only compensate for the shortness of the stanza by their added weight but also contribute to the majesty of the whole. Handled with less control and feeling, this poem might have resulted in mere bathos and hollow rhetoric, but Robinson's restraint, sincerity, and sure skill make it a triumphant work of art.

"Three Quatrains" is composed in one of the simplest stanza forms in English: four pentameter lines with alternating rhyme. The movement is simple and straightforward. Stanza one introduces the theme of fame and glory in general terms; stanza two cites two examples; stanza three makes a general application. Within each quatrain and through the poem as a whole, there are nice gradations of tone, from the high commanding opening tone of "Fame's imperious music" to the all-too-earthy "Glory weighs itself in dust," at the end of the first stanza, and the "withered leaf in every laurel" at the end of the poem. Subtle alliteration and assonance and verbal links and contrasts contribute both music and strength. The feminine ending in the second rhyme of the last stanza coincides musically with thought and image to intensify the effect of fading away that is the theme of the poem. It is not surprising if "Three Quatrains" is reminiscent of the past, for it is written in the same style and form as Gray's famous "Elegy." Robinson himself could not have been unaware of this fact. In December 1894 Robinson sent the first stanza of "Three Quatrains" to Harry Smith with the comment that it was "a little experimental quatrain in the 'grand style.' " There is, of course, no such thing as a single grand style in English in any sense that can be defined specifically, though there is a sense in which the term is meaningful. There are as many potential grand styles as there are poets. Shakespeare's grand style is not Milton's. Each spoke in his own voice, though not always in the grand style. The grand style is not solely a matter of diction nor of form; nor is it merely a combination of these, though both play a part in it. Nor is it a thing of the past only, though the past plays a part in it too. The grand style, if it means anything, is the use of language in which thought and emotion are heightened and fused and given significance by the theme, by alive and meaningful words of appropriate dignity arranged rhythmically in a structurally unified form, and by the sincerity of the poet. All of these components are necessary. The cumulative resources of the language each poet has at his disposal. Whether he makes use of them or not depends upon his intelligence, sensitivity, and technical skill. As an imitative poem "Three Quatrains" is successful, but it is not completely Robinson's own voice. It is of interest, however, for several reasons. It illustrates again Robinson's technical skill even as a beginner, reveals once more his sense of a continuing relationship between the past and the present, and indicates his conscious efforts to extend his command of language.

In striking contrast to "Three Quatrains" is "The Clerks." Here Robinson speaks in his authentic voice, though not in his grand style. The form is conventional, a sonnet, but the treatment is unconventional both in language and in material. "There is poetry in all types of humanity," Robinson had said. Even in clerks. The language, especially in the octave, is prosy, close to that of ordinary conversation, mainly words of one syllable; the tone is pitched low at the beginning but rises in the sestet.

> I did not think that I should find them there
> When I came back again, but there they stood,

he begins. It sounds like an offhand comment that one could jot down as fast as it could be spoken, yet Robinson "tinkered" with the poem for a month before he was satisfied. The theme of the poem is not so much the vanity of seekers after fame or glory as it is that no man, regardless of his ambition or his position, should consider himself superior to others; for all men are one in being both human and mortal. The poem is built on the initial contrast and later identification of the seemingly lowly clerks and others who either aspire to great heights ("ache so much to be sublime") or who are proud of their high social position because of their lineage (their "descent"). The impact of the poem is a delayed one which many readers miss because they disregard the manner of presentation, especially the point of view from which the poem is given and the almost submerged imagery and symbolism. The poem is the recounting of a dramatic incident of great import to the narrator. The scene is a drygoods store to which the narrator has returned after an absence of some years. He is surprised to see the same clerks who were there before, grown old doing the same job day after day, taking down bolts of yardgoods from the shelves, measuring it out by the ell, cutting it off, and putting the bolts back in tiers on the shelves. The narrator's attitude of surprise identifies him with the groups in the sestet and reveals his initial sense of superiority. Like the goods left too long on the shelf or on display, the clerks have become shopworn and hence reduced in value, he feels. The narrator's moment of insight comes in the recognition of their essential humanity, and as he observes them at work their simple task takes on symbolic significance: the ell, the unit of measurement of cloth, becomes a unit of time, "the alnage of the years," to which all men are subject. Poets, kings, and clerks are all brought together in the final three lines, where Robinson welds them into an indissoluble union not only by the imagery but by strong metrical ties as well. For those familiar with the Greek concept of the three Fates, the poem takes on an extra dimension. It is instructive also to compare Robinson's earlier "Supremacy," which is similar in theme, to see how far he had come in four years. It was first published in *The Harvard Advocate* on June 16, 1892, in the following form:

> There is a drear and lonely tract of Hell
>> From all the common gloom removed afar:
>> A flat, sad land where only shadows are,
> Whose lorn estate no word of mine can tell.
> I walked among the shades and knew them well:
>> Men I had scorned upon Life's little star
>> For churls and sluggards; and I knew the scar
> Upon their brows of woe ineffable.
>
> But as I moved triumphant on my way,
>> Into the dark they vanished, one by one.
> Then came an awful light, a blinding ray —
>> As if a new creation were begun;
> And with a swift, importunate dismay,
>> I heard the dead men singing in the sun.

Even though Robinson improved "Supremacy" considerably, for inclusion in his first volume, it remains much inferior to "The Clerks." In "The Clerks" Robinson not only invested the common-place with significance but also gave to the anemic sonnet of his time a blood transfusion that restored it to its former vigor.

Time is only one aspect of man's existence. Man lives in time, but he also has a relationship to an infinitely larger Power. The way man views the universe has a bearing on the way he lives, or ought to live, his everyday life. Conversely, a man's daily existence is to some extent a reflection of his philosophy. In most of the remaining poems in *The Children of the Night* Robinson was directly concerned with man and his relationship to the universe. In such poems as "Credo," "The Altar," "The Garden," "Dead Village," "The Torrent," "The World," "Kosmos," "Two sonnets," "The Children of the Night," "Octaves," and "L'Envoi" he explored various aspects of this topic. His idealistic philosophy runs throughout these poems: his conception of an ordered and purposeful universe founded in wisdom and in love, the necessity of self-knowledge, and the futility of materialism. When Harry Smith first read *The Torrent and The Night Before,* he complained that some of the poems were too personal and too "damned didactic." Smith's criticism had some validity; occasionally, as in "Kosmos," Robinson used bare statement and abstractions supported only by a hortatory tone instead of rendering idea and emotion in poetic terms. In most of these poems, however, the themes are carried by threads of music-light-dark imagery, and in "Octaves" they are loosely woven together to form a kind of poetic tapestry illustrative of Robinson's thought. These themes and images, especially the light-dark opposition, Robinson would continue to explore from various points of view and with increasing penetration for the rest of his life. By the end of January 1898 the book that Louise Bogan has called "one of the hinges upon which American poetry was able to turn ·from the sentimentality of the nineties toward modern veracity and psychological truth" and which Allen Tate said "marks the beginning of a new era in American poetry" had, with the help of the Christmas trade, sold a total of three hundred copies. But by that time Robinson was already full of ideas for another book.

Robinson at this time was twenty-eight. Daniel Gregory Mason, whom he met in the spring of 1899, described him as "tall and in a sensitive way handsome, with dark, fine hair, flowing moustache, and fresh healthy color. Beautiful were his large and peculiarly limpid dark eyes. They gleamed and glowed behind his spectacles, alternately quiet with poetic penetration and dancing with humorous irony." He had gone to New York to get away from what had become an intolerable state of affairs: the family situation was painful; the people of Gardiner, he felt, regarded him as "an unpromising freak and a queer cuss without ambition,"; his nerves were taut "like the E string of a fiddle." He needed, as he said a bit later, "the biggest conglomeration of humanity and inhumanity that America affords. . . ." His good friend George Burnham was in New York, and there he would be close to the pulse of the literary world. He was following the advice he had given to Edith Brower: "The thing for you to do is to go right down into the middle of life and compel the world to feel . . . the tension of endeavor, the pathos of failure & success. . . ." From this time on, except for two periods in 1898 and 1899 when he was first in Gardiner, then in Cambridge, Robinson regarded New York as his permanent residence.

Even before *The Children of the Night* was published Robinson had mentioned another book of a different sort that he had to get out of his system. In January 1898 he began work on a long blankverse poem that eventually became "The Book of Annandale." He felt that he was in a "transition stage," and that his new work was "an entirely new departure." He had reservations about some of his earlier work — the Hardy sonnet, "Oh for a poet," and "The Night Before," for example — and he was conscious of the didacticism that Smith had complained of in *The Children of the Night*. His next work, he told Miss Brower, would not be "preachy." In March he put the first book aside temporarily to work on a second, again of an entirely different sort. In June, back in Gardiner, he had an idea for another poem; it would be humorous, "about two old men." Later he would name them — Isaac and Archibald. Shortly afterward he was composing "The Old Maid," which he later entitled "Aunt Imogen." It is notable that all of these turned out to be longish narrative poems, ranging from 150 to 500 lines, with the emphasis on character analysis. Then early in 1899 Robinson began what was to be his most extended study to date of the "pathos of failure & success." It was "about a pauper," he wrote Miss Brower, ". . . and will be a sort of human development of the octaves. It will disgust and frighten some people, and, I hope, please others." The poem was "Captain Craig." By mid-may 1900 it was completed. To Harry Smith, the poet wrote that the new book was "a rather particular kind of twentieth century comedy."

Robinson completed "Captain Craig" just as William Vaughn Moody's "An Ode in Time of Hesitation" was published in the *Atlantic Monthly*. A passionate denunciation of United States policy in the Philippines, this poem struck the moral conscience of the nation. *The Masque of Judgment,* "Gloucester Moors," "On a Soldier Fallen in the Philippines," and *Poems* all appeared within a year. Moody's star was in the ascendant, and it continued to rise throughout the decade, while Robinson's remained mostly hidden. There is a strange irony in the relationship of these two men. Always Moody shone, while Robinson remained in the background. Born in the same year, they both attended Harvard, where Moody was a brilliant scholar and literary light, while Robinson was a "special student" whose poems made *The Harvard Advocate* but not the more prestigious *Harvard Monthly;* Moody remained as a graduate assistant and then went on to a career of scholarship and teaching at the University of Chicago, while Robinson went home to Gardiner. Robinson did have a job at Harvard from January to June 1899. Through the efforts of John Hays Gardiner, he was made a confidential clerk in the office of President Eliot, a job that Robinson described as "a sort of assistant secretary and metaphorical bottle washer to the whole concern." After six months Robinson told the college officials that he was in the wrong place and they agreed with him. Moody went on from success to success, while Robinson's pattern seemed to be only a succession of failures. Few would have predicted that within a decade after Moody's death their respective positions would be reversed.

Robinson and Moody became acquainted through a mutual friend, Daniel Gregory Mason, musician and writer, whom Robinson had met while working at Harvard. Different as the two poets were in temperament, manner, and taste, Robinson and Moody became friends — and poetic rivals. Both of them were attempting to write poetry that would deal significantly with the realities of a new age, but the paths they were following were not the same. Robinson was acutely aware of the differences between Moody's approach and his own. When he learned that Moody was writing a masque, he regretted it and told Moody he thought his "proper field" was "in the breathing realities of common life." Eventually he came to regard *The Masque of Judgment* as "a pretty big thing." He wrote to John Hays Gardiner that Moody had taken "most difficult and unpromising material" and "vitalized it according to modern methods" and "made a modern poem of it." But he also wrote to Josephine Preston Peabody that Moody's greatest trouble lay in the fact that he had "so many things to unlearn." Although he said that Moody's "An Ode in Time of Hesitation" was "a stunning piece of work . . . in the spirit of the new age," he was sorry that that it was called an ode and could not help thinking that Moody was "still given to what [John Hays] Gardiner calls an 'occasional affectation of vocabulary.'" Although Robinson preferred "Gloucester Moors" to the "more splendiferous ode," his reaction to its diction was one of intense dislike, and he frankly said so to Moody: "But I beseech you to agree with [me] in showering all sorts of damnation on your occasional, inconsistent and obnoxious use of archaic monstrosities like 'lifteth,' 'doth,' etc. I may be narrow and unreasonable on this point, but I am pretty confident that in ten years from now this sort of thing will not be tolerated." Robinson could not help comparing his own work with that of Moody. Writing to Josephine Preston Peabody, he said Moody's *Masque* "makes me feel funny with my *Captain Craigs,* etc., but I take comfort in the fact that the books are so ridiculously different that a comparison is hardly possible." But Moody's poetry was published and Robinson's was not. *Captain Craig* went the rounds of five publishing houses before it finally was published, in October 1902, by Moody's publisher, Houghton Mifflin. It was accepted reluctantly "on commission," with the assurance that the cost would be underwritten by John Hays Gardiner and, unknown to Robinson, by Laura E. Richards of Gardiner, Maine. After so long a time, to Robinson its publication was an anticlimax.

The hopes that Robinson had had in coming to New York had gradually dwindled. No matter what he did, his poetry was unacceptable to the editors. The constant rebuffs had worn him down. Though there were a few perceptive reviews of *Captain Craig,* most of them were negative, and the few words of praise were for some of the shorter, conventional poems in the volume. He had been able to manage financially for the first few years in New York on funds received periodically from the estate, but now he was in serious straits. He was living in a narrow hall-bedroom on the fourth floor of a rooming house on West 23rd Street. He was behind in his rent, his clothes were worn, he was eating in the cheapest restaurants he could find. He had friends who had faith in him and who occasionally gave him money, but it rankled him to have to take it, and it did not solve his problem. He withdrew into himself, living an existence that became increasingly lonely. In the fall of 1903 he took a job as time-checker in the construction of the New York subway. The work was not difficult, but it was tedious and the tunnels were damp and gaseous. He worked ten hours a day for two dollars. Physically and emotionally exhausted, he was drinking heavily. Though he received temporary solace from alcohol, he paid a price for it; it took him years to overcome his addiction. The subway job lasted until August 1904. In January 1905 Robinson's friend William E. Butler, who had financed the publication of *The Children of the Night,* offered him a part-time job in the advertising department of his drygoods store in Boston; he would have some time to write. Robinson accepted. Then in March 1905 he received a letter from the President of the United States. It was a major turning point in the poet's life. Again he was indebted to the Richards family. Henry Richards was teaching at the Groton School, where he introduced young Kermit Roosevelt to Robinson's *The Children of the Night.* The boy conveyed his enthusiasm to his father, who in turn wrote to Robinson: "I have enjoyed your poems, especially 'The Children of the Night' so much that I must write to tell you so. Will you permit me to ask what you are doing and how you are getting along? I wish I could see you." After some correspondence and backstage maneuvering, a position was made for Robinson; he was given a place in the United States Customs Service in New York as a special agent of the Treasury Department. It was a sinecure. "I want you to understand," the President told Robinson, "that I expect you to think poetry first and Treasury second." At the instigation of Roosevelt, Scribner's took over *The Children of the Night.* The President wrote a review of it in *The Outlook,* commenting that "There is an undoubted touch of genius in the poems. . . ." In October the Scribner edition was published. Robinson, writing to Kermit Roosevelt many years later, summed up what the President's assistance meant to him: "I don't like to think of where I should be now if it had not been for your astonishing father. He fished me out of hell by the hair of the head."

4

1906~1935: A Summary

In our discussion of the environment in which E. A. Robinson grew up, the formative personal and literary influences, and his early work, the groundwork basic to an understanding of the poet's mind and art has been laid. It remains now to survey the most significant events in Robinson's life from this point on before turning to an examination of his poetry.

The period 1906–1913 was Robinson's dramatic interlude. A single volume of poety, *The Town Down the River,* was published in 1910. He spent most of the time writing plays, rewriting the plays as novels, and finally reshaping the plays for publication and possible production. Two prose plays were published: *Van Zorn* in 1914 and *The Porcupine in* 1915. Only *Van Zorn* was ever produced; staged by the Brooklyn Community Theatre Company, it had a week's run at the local Y.M.C.A. in February 1917. That Robinson at this stage of his career should have had an affair with drama may seem more like a strange interlude than anything else. Like Miniver Cheevy, he had his reasons.

For years American drama had been in the doldrums. Adaptations of novels, translations of foreign plays, and sentimental melodramas were the staples of the stage; elaborate sets and costumes

provided spectacle and glamour. Of original and creative work,
there was practically nothing. But the same winds of change that
had begun to stir the dead calm of poetry had also begun to liven
the theater. Four of Robinson's friends were playing a vital part in
this change: Percy MacKaye, Ridgely Torrence, Josephine Preston
Peabody, and William Vaughn Moody. Poet-dramatists, they all
had a vision of a "Poets' Theatre in America." Not that they
thought plays must be written in verse, though some of them did
write in verse; rather, they believed that plays should be poetic in
conception. Percy MacKaye was the most vociferous spokesman,
but it was Moody who made the most smashing hit with his *The
Great Divide*. A milestone in the development of American drama,
it opened in New York in October 1906 and had a phenomenally
successful run of more than a thousand performances. The enthusiasm of these playwrights was contagious, and Robinson caught
it. His poem "The White Lights" clearly indicates the perspective
in which he saw the movement as a whole:

> When in from Delos came the gold
> That held the dream of Pericles,
> When first Athenian ears were told
> The tumult of Euripides,
> When men met Aristophanes,
> Who fledged them with immortal quills —
> Here, where the time knew none of these,
> There were some islands and some hills.
>
> When Rome went ravening to see
> The sons of mothers end their days,
> When Flaccus bade Leuconoë
> To banish her Chaldean ways,
> When first the pearled, alembic phrase
> Of Maro into music ran —
> Here there was neither blame nor praise
> For Rome, or for the Mantuan.
>
> When Avon, like a faery floor,
> Lay freighted, for the eyes of One,
> With galleons laden long before
> By moonlit wharves in Avalon —

Here, where the white lights have begun
To seethe a way for something fair,
No prophet knew, from what was done,
That there was triumph in the air.

From the classical dramatists of Greece and Rome, to Shakespeare, to contemporary Broadway. There is no doubt, too, that Robinson desired the satisfying sense of recognition that comes with real success. Theodore Roosevelt's praise of his poetry had been sweet indeed, and it had opened some editorial doors that had hitherto been closed to him, but his latest book of new poems, *Captain Craig,* had not been well received. Drama offered exciting possibilities in which to record other "scattered lives." By January 1907 Robinson had completed the first draft of *Ferguson's Ivory Tower,* later entitled *Van Zorn;* he had also done a one-act play entitled *Terra Firma,* no longer extant. By October he had finished *The Porcupine.* Moody thought the latter "a stunning play" and attempted to interest Broadway producer Charles Frohman in it but was unsuccessful.

As long as Robinson had his job, money was not the pressing problem that it had been. However, he was helping to support his brother Herman's family also, and after 1909 money did make a difference. In February of that year Herman died, alone, in a Boston hospital.[1] In March, Roosevelt went out of office; shortly afterward, Robinson went out of his office also at the request of the new administration. The persistence with which Robinson attempted in one way or another to salvage the plays reflects both his dogged determination and the financial pressure he felt. By March 1913 he had to admit that he could not "hit the popular chord," that when he tried to "write for the crowd" he perpetrated "the damnedest rubbish that you ever heard of. . . ." He was going to write another book of poems.

Meanwhile *The Town Down the River,* published three years earlier, was beginning to make its way. With this volume Robinson came to full maturity. Both stronger and more restrained than his previous volumes, it reveals a poet detached yet sympathetic and in full control of his craft. A collection of thirty-one short poems,

[1] C. P. Smith reports that after Herman's death, Robinson proposed marriage to Emma at least three times: late in 1909, in 1918, and in 1928.

it contains some of his finest work. The same strong ethical note is here, but the preachy tone is gone. In "The Master," a tribute to Lincoln, and in "The Revealer," a tribute to Theodore Roosevelt to whom the book was dedicated, Robinson exhibits a social consciousness that foreshadows much of his later work. Throughout there is greater subtlety: subtlety of situation, as in the puzzling "How Annandale Went Out" and in "The Whip," a cryptic poem with a form as taut as its subject; and subtlety of tone, as in the delicate shadings and modulations of "For a Dead Lady," one of Robinson's finest lyrics.

In the summer of 1911, at the suggestion of Hermann Hagedorn, Robinson went to the MacDowell Colony in Peterborough, New Hampshire, an institution designed to give creative artists an opportunity to carry on their work away from the distractions of the city. Set among hills covered with laurel and hemlock, with a view of Mount Monadnock in the distance, it was an ideal spot for uninterrupted creative work. Robinson, wary of organized groups and activities of any kind, went reluctantly. He became the Colony's most distinguished resident, returning every summer for the rest of his life. Thus began a cyclical pattern which provided change and regularity and which became Robinson's working schedule: Peterborough in the summer, June through September, writing his poems; New York the rest of the year, revising his poems, reading proof, attending the theater and concerts, seeing friends, getting new ideas to work into poems at the Colony. Going and coming, it was his practice to stop off in Boston to see friends. Financial worries lessened as the years went by. In 1914 his devoted friend and loyal supporter, John Hays Gardiner, died and left him a bequest of $4,000; in 1917 a group of anonymous friends established a trust fund of $1,200 a year which was at Robinson's disposal as long as he needed it. With housing also provided by friends in New York, Robinson was free to devote himself to his poetry.

Robinson's decision to return to poetry came at about the same time that Ezra Pound and Robert Frost were discussing the merits of *The Town Down the River* in England, where Frost himself hoped to find a more responsive audience for his poetry. But by then it was already becoming apparent to Robinson and others in the United States that poetry here was no longer getting a chilly reception. The smoldering of the nineties and the flickerings of the first decade of the century, fed by the spirit of the new age, had finally burst into flame. The glow was felt throughout the nation. In the arts, increased creative activity resulted in increased outlets for expression. Led by Harriet Monroe's *Poetry: A Magazine of Verse,* little magazines devoted to poetry sprang up across the country. Poetry at last had an opportunity to get a hearing, and poets wanted to be heard. Robinson was heard too, though many were surprised to learn that he had been speaking for some time. With the publication of *The Man Against the Sky* in 1916, it was clear that here was a poet of stature at the height of his powers.

Robinson's reaction to the experimentation and theorizing that characterized the period was one of interest, sometimes of amusement, and at times of dismay. Suddenly, it seemed, poetry was a game that anyone could play, and each player made up his own set of rules. Manifestoes were issued like royal proclamations, each giving the last word as to what was poetry and what was not: Imagism, Objectivism, Vorticism, Symbolism — each had its own theory. Verbal battles were fought in the pages of the little magazines, and none more bitterly than the controversy over free verse. Freedom was equated with originality and the two together with modernity, but too often freedom became license and originality mere novelty. When William Stanley Braithwaite interviewed Robinson for the *Boston Evening Transcript* in May 1913, he asked him what he thought the "character and quality of the poetry shaping itself" for the growing interest in the humanities would be. Robinson replied:

> I don't know anything about the poetry of the future, except that it must have, in order to be poetry, the same eternal and unchangeable quality of magic that it has always had. Of course, it must always be colored by the age and the individual, but the thing itself will always remain unmistakable and indefinable. It seems to me a great deal of time and effort is now wasted in trying to make poetry do what it was never intended to do.

In replying to Amy Lowell's congratulatory letter about *The Man Against the Sky,* Robinson took the opportunity to remind her that what seems to me to be the very best of your *vers libre* is almost exclusively "human" in its subject matter, and therefore substantially old-fashioned. One reason why I haven't more to say on the subject is that I have absolutely no theories. I don't care a pinfeather what form a poem is written in so long as it makes me sit up. "Imagiste" work, *per se*, taken as a theory apart from one special form, seems to me rather too self-conscious and exclusive to stand the test of time. I feel pretty confident that if you had to sacrifice one or the other you would retain that part of your poetry that has in it the good and bad solid old-fashioned human qualities that make us all one crazy family of children, throwing things at each other across the table, and making faces at each other *in saecula saeculorum*.

What Robinson objected to in the experimental writing was the technical flabbiness of much of the work and the obvious efforts to be different, even to the point of being bizarre. "The test of time" — always Robinson thought of himself as part of a continuing and flexible tradition in which technique and vision were both necessary if a poem was to last. The forms that had been handed down and modified through the generations were still sufficiently plastic for his needs. To Lucius Beebe he stated his position clearly and pointedly: "I am essentially a classicist in poetic composition, and I believe that the accepted media for the masters of the past will continue to be used in the future. There is, of course, room for infinite variety, manipulation and invention within the limits of traditional forms and meters, but any violent deviation from the classic mean may be a confession of inability to do the real thing, poetically speaking." In that simple phrase, "the real thing," the essential integrity of Robinson the artist shines forth; his life was built on it.

On June 28, 1914, a shot at Serajevo plunged the world into war. Robinson saw the war as an extreme manifestation of materialism — materialism carried to its logical, destructive end. This is the main or subordinate theme of a number of major poems written in the context of World War I. As one by one, in the summer of 1914, the countries of Europe were drawn into the maelstrom, the United States congratulated itself on its neutrality; at the same time it maintained its right to sell and ship contraband of war, and it welcomed the opportunity to make loans to the belligerents, especially since the proceeds were invested in the United States for the purchase of food and military supplies. In "Cassandra," with vitriolic irony, Robinson, using a fictive evangelist as his spokesman, warned a complacent nation of the consequences of operating on a system of inverted values, in which "Your Dollar is your only Word." "The Man Against the Sky," more profound than "Cassandra" and broader in scope, was precipitated by the war, which serves as a backdrop to the larger drama of the poem. With the publication of *Merlin* (1917) and *Lancelot* (1920), some who formerly had praised Robinson as a pioneer in modern American poetry felt betrayed because they thought he had turned his back on the contemporary world. Both poems were written during the war, and the more astute readers were fully aware of the contemporary significance of the legendary material.

The comparative neglect of the early years was balanced by the high respect accorded Robinson in his later years. On December 21, 1919, *The New York Times Review of Books* devoted its first page to a celebration of Robinson's fiftieth birthday with tributes from seventeen friends and fellow poets. Professor Bliss Perry of Harvard saw Robinson's work as "uncompromising, consistent, integral." Arthur Davison Ficke commented that "His curiously penetrating insight into the labyrinths of the mind and his scrupulous artistic integrity have always been a delight and an inspiration to the rest of us. He is beyond the reach of fad or fashion." Along with others, Edgar Lee Masters acknowledged the pioneer nature of the poet's work: "Mr. Robinson was producing poetry of importance in one of the most sterile periods of American history. . . . He has had the good fortune to live to this day of recognition of his work, both for its own value and as an expression of today." The publication in 1921 of the *Collected Poems,* eight volumes to date, became the occasion for an overall assessment of Robinson's work. It met with critical acclaim across the nation, and Robinson received the Pulitzer award, an honor to be twice repeated. In 1922 the *Collected Poems* appeared in England with an introduction by poet-dramatist John Drinkwater; in an address to the Royal Society of Literature, Drinkwater referred to Robinson as "one of the six greatest poets writing today." In 1922 Yale conferred on Robinson an honorary degree of Doctor of Letters; Bowdoin did likewise three years later. *Tristram,* published in 1927, brought Robinson into the public limelight. The Literary Guild of America selected it for distribution to its members, and accompanied it with a book-length essay on Robinson by Mark Van Doren. The book was launched by a public reception at the Little Theatre, where Mrs. August Belmont (the former Eleanor Robson, an actress) read passages to an enthusiastic audience that crowded into the building. In addition to the Literary Guild edition, *Tristram* went through twenty printings in the first year, with sales of more than 50,000 copies. Pleased as he was, Robinson refused to be lionized.

The end of the war brought prohibition and the bootlegger, fast cars and flappers, easy money and easy virtue, and many other things. A superficial gaiety pervaded the atmosphere, but in the distance, hardly audible above the din, were sullen rumblings of the coming depression and of another storm gathering. This was the generation that got lost, the time when T. S. Eliot created Gerontion, Sinclair Lewis gave being to Babbitt, and Scott Fitzgerald begat Gatsby. It was the age that gave birth to these characters; it was the percipience of the authors that made them symbolic. Serious writers, and other people as well, were very much concerned about the headlong pace of a hellbent society. E. A. Robinson was gravely concerned also, and his concern shows up repeatedly in the poems of this period as well as in his personal letters. The enactment of the eighteenth amendment to the Constitution, Robinson took as an affront to personal liberty, the first step that might lead to further restrictions of individual freedom. He took a sharp look at the country and the people. The tendency toward conformity, with the consequent loss of individuality, the power of big business and the machine to control the lives of people, the equating of equality and mediocrity with democracy, filled him with dismay. The results of this study of "miscalled democracy" he put into "Dionysius in Doubt" and "Demos and Dionysius," two poems that come as close to propaganda as any that Robinson ever wrote. In "Tasker Norcross," his "nonentity poem," he drew a picture of the barren life of a man without faith or philosophy. The uncertain state of world affairs and the necessity of laying new foundations for peace based on moral principles, he dealt with in "The Old King's New Jester" and "The Garden of the Nations." The background of these poems and many of the long narrative poems that make up the bulk of Robinson's later work is that of those troubled times. Rarely, however, does it obtrude, for Robinson was not concerned with specific, isolated events but rather with the general ethical climate and the relationships of people. Yet his letters reveal how closely he followed contemporary events and his prophetic awareness of the dangerous direction they were taking. As early as March 1919 he wrote to Mrs. Mabel Dodge Sterne, "Meanwhile we shall have the League of Nations to play with while Germany is getting herself and Russia together for another grand smash. You will see from this that I have no faith in any social scheme that doesn't see beyond a moonshine millennium." To Mrs. Laura E. Richards, with whom Robinson had been corresponding for more than thirty years, he wrote in the spring of 1930 that he was glad to be in Boston and "out of New York, which is altogether too good a symbol of this after the war world, which I don't like at all at all. So far as I can see it must get worse and worse until it busts. . . ." Again to Mrs. Richards in December 1932, nine years before Pearl Harbor, he wrote: "Japan is the world's hornet's nest, and will keep on buzzing and stinging for some hundreds of years — so far as we can see. I haven't liked this world since 1914 — which means perhaps that I am growing old inside." And in February 1934: "Today I have been thinking of Hitler, and of what one neurotic fanatic may yet do to us and drag us into. It's all right to say it can't happen, but unfortunately it can."

After the triumph of *Tristram,* which Robinson had written with intense intellectual and emotional excitement, he continued to write a volume nearly every year, all long narrative poems except for *Nicodemus* (1932). He turned sixty in 1929 just after the stock-market crash and the beginning of the depression. Friends have attributed his compulsion to keep on writing to worry lest he become again financially dependent. One must add, however, that ever since 1893 when he first sat down to record in his book the record of the "scattered lives" of those he observed, Robinson had been a writer. He continued to do what he was born to do. But there was a definite slowing down in his last few years. At the end of each summer's work he was a bit more tired. First there was just weariness, then in the fall of 1934 a series of headaches, then severe inner pain. Taken to the New York Hospital in January for what he thought was phlebitis, it was discovered that he had inoperable cancer of the pancreas. Robinson had just time to complete the reading of proof for his last major work, *King Jasper,* a symbolic poem about a crumbling world. Characteristically, it ended on a note of hope. On April 6, 1935, Robinson died. At his funeral, his coffin was covered with branches from the woods adjacent to his studio at the MacDowell Colony — branches of hemlock and, most appropriately, of laurel.

5

Robinson's Poetry:
Characteristics and Illustrations

Over a period of forty years E. A. Robinson wrote twenty volumes of poetry. What is surprising is not the quantity but the high quality of so much of it. In his later years, to be sure, Robinson wrote too much too fast, and in general the later poems, especially after *Tristram,* are not up to the level of his earlier work, but this is not to say that they do not have an interest of their own. His work as a whole shows a definite pattern of development. His basic philosophic position remains unchanged throughout, and he treats essentially the same themes; the development occurs in depth and in breadth. With a few exceptions, the early poems, up to 1916, are short poems written in a variety of conventional forms handled with great flexibility; they consist of brief character sketches, miniature dramas, and concise reflective pieces. Poems of medium length, such as "Isaac and Archibald" and "The Book of Annandale," and the lengthy "Captain Craig" anticipate the long poems that dominate the later period. Beginning with *Merlin* in 1917, most of the later work consists of long narrative poems written in blank verse, which deal with larger individual and social issues and contain much psychological probing. The movement of Robinson's work is from a small canvas to a large one, and increasingly from outer to inner treatment of character and situation. Though Robinson did write a number of fine short poems later in life — "The Wandering Jew," "The Mill," "Mr. Flood's Party," and "The Sheaves," for example — the tendency toward more extended and complicated works grew out of something deep in Robinson. Esther Bates, who closely observed the poet at work over a period of years, reports that "Once, during his later years, he said sadly, 'People ask me why I do not do the short poems any more. I can't. They don't come any more. At least, not good ones. And I'm not willing to publish poems I know are inferior to the early ones.' He was silent for a few moments. Then he said again, 'They don't come any more.' " Unfortunately, many people know Robinson's work only through anthological snippets; unfamiliar with the longer works, they thus have a limited view of the range and scope of his work as a whole.

One day when Robinson was attending one of Mrs. MacDowell's teas at the Colony, three beaming but determined women in wedge formation bore down upon him and backed him into a corner. "I just adore your poetry," said one of the ladies; "in fact, we all do. But it is so hard to understand. I wish you would tell us some easy way." To which the poet replied, "I don't know that there is any — except just to read it one word after another." To a naive question, a simple answer.

A poem is the product of an age and an individual. Time and place, culture and language, elements that enter into the composition of a poem (or any work of art) even without the poet's awareness, enable us to distinguish with some degree of accuracy the work of one period from that of another. But what distinguishes the work of one writer from another in a given period is the mind and temperament of the creator himself. T. S. Eliot, Robert Frost, and E. A. Robinson share certain characteristics common to our age, but their work is clearly differentiated by a style that is in each case unique. The style is the man, the stamp of character. It is this that enables us on hearing a poem — or a symphony or a story — to identify it as Shakespeare or Beethoven or Faulkner. Or Robinson. But such a recognition is not based on a single characteristic, nor does it come as the result of knowing a single work. Rather it is based on a complex of characteristics that one has come to know through wide acquaintance with the work of the author.

Robinson is not an easy poet, but the difficulties of reading him have been exaggerated. He is less difficult than Yeats or Eliot, though equally profound. He uses no esoteric symbols, nor does he have a mythical world of his own that requires exegesis. His forms are generally open and straightforward, and his language is that of cultured speech used with precision. The purpose of art is to clarify, not to obscure, and Robinson is never purposely obscure. Indeed, it should be perfectly clear that he wanted above all else to communicate. His poems were written, as he said in different ways a number of times, "with a conscious hope that they might make some despairing devil a little stronger and a little better satisfied with things — not as they are, but as they are to be." A poet "if he is to be anything," he said, must be "an interpreter of life." Set five painters down in one spot and ask them to paint the same scene and you will get five different pictures, each one a valid interpretation. How successful each is as a work of art will depend on how well the artist can render in moving and convincing form what he sees, either with his outer or his inner eye. The same is true of poets except that they use words instead of paint. But what an artist sees and how he treats it form together his interpretation; both derive from the uniqueness of the mind and temperament of the artist.

Robinson was by nature restrained and reticent; though kind and understanding, he was not given to outward show of emotion. Nor was he in his poetry interested in describing his own personal emotions, though many of his poems had their origin in deeply felt personal experiences. As an interpreter of life, he wanted to portray life as truthfully and objectively as he could. He knew, however, that there is no such thing as complete objectivity in art and that art and life are two different things. What an artist must do, he said, is to give the illusion of life. There are many ways of achieving this. One way is by specificity, the piling up of details to attain a realistic effect, as in the work of Theodore Dreiser or Sinclair Lewis. This is not Robinson's method. He was not interested in exterior realism, but in states of mind, the inter-action of people, the consequences of actions. The people who interested him primarily were the failures, the misfits, the troubled; people in the wrong jobs, people with the wrong marital partner, people with the wrong goals. Success that fails and failure that succeeds, the disparity between appearance and reality — these are dominant themes. It is a world of incongruity and paradox, the foundations of irony and humor which can blend into pathos or poignance. It is an inner world to be reached only by indirec-tion. And Robinson's method is one of indirection. It requires subtlety, careful selection of details, and control; and it demands a sensitive alertness of the reader. Carried too far, such an approach results in obscurity, and occasionally Robinson is guilty of this. More often than not, however, the reader has failed to note some significant detail that Robinson has carefully dropped along the way. "The Mill," "The Whip," and "How Annandale Went Out," all short poems, are excellent examples of Robinson's indirect treatment.

"The Mill" is a miniature drama in twenty-four lines, obliquely presented by hints and suggestion. Understatement is the keynote. What happened is never explicitly stated, though it becomes clear, if we follow closely, that there has been a double suicide because "There are no millers any more." Details casually introduced in-duce a mood of doubt and foreboding: the long wait, the cold tea, the dead fire, "there might *yet* be nothing wrong / In *how he went*," the lingering at the door. Everything in the first stanza takes on significance and becomes emotionally charged in the light of the wife's discovery, in the second stanza, of the miller's body. The general statement that "There are no millers any more" was not strictly true when spoken, for it did not include the miller himself. But the lines

> What else there was would only seem
> To say again what he had meant

reveal the reason for his suicide and make the original statement now true in fact. The mill's "warm / And mealy fragrance of the past" contrasts sharply with the second line of the first stanza and makes it strongly ironic, for more than the tea was cold, more than the fire was dead. It also makes it symbolic, the tea and fire becoming symbols of domesticity and life as well as an unbearable present, now cold and dead because the miller's occupation and the miller himself are gone. The cumulative force of the whole is sufficient explanation of the wife's drowning herself. Nowhere does Robinson describe the troubled state of mind of the wife, but it is there nonetheless in the ambiguity of "She may have reasoned in the dark" and in the superb last four lines, in which the untroubled water, an inverted heaven ("starry velvet"), softly closes over her. The strict regularity of the meter is interrupted only twice: once at "Sick with a fear" to reflect the wife's apprehensiveness, and once, with a double stress, at "Black water" to accentuate the finality of her act.

"The Whip" is a much more cryptic poem, about which there has been considerable debate. A drama of a triangular relationship, it concerns a husband who commits suicide when he confirms his suspicions that his wife has been unfaithful to him, and when he discovers that she not only does not love him but hates him. A narrator, presumably a friend who has known of the situation, attends the funeral. Through his thoughts, a "conversation" with the dead man, the situation is gradually revealed as he tries to understand why the husband should take his own life. We are not told that the triangle involves a husband and wife; the three are referred to as "the mistress," "the slave," and "the lover." Since the one who is dead was tyrannized, he must be the slave. We gather that "the mistress" is his wife because she is unlike "The roses and the sod" that "Will not forswear the wave"; she has, in other words, forsworn her marriage oath. As wife, she is mistress of her slave-husband, but she is also mistress, in the illicit sense, to the lover. The affair, we gather, had gone on for some time, the husband fighting all the time to believe his suspicions unfounded. Finally, he laid plans to catch them ("The cynic net you cast"). He permitted the two to go off together, presumably on horseback, "to find / Their own way to the brink." When after a chase he came upon them, he "chose to plunge and sink" in the river below. In stanza one, we learn that the husband is dead and are given the reasons, though they are at this point not clear; in stanza two, we find out that he drowned; in stanza three that he chose to drown when his plot succeeded. At this point the narrator asks, "shall I call you blind?", with the implication that he was indeed blind, that he should not have committed suicide, especially since he had merely confirmed what he probably had known for a long time. It is not until the narrator observes the welt on the dead man's face that he understands what happened. As the husband at the end of his chase approached the couple, the wife turned and struck him with her riding whip. When the narrator at the end of the poem again asks, "Still, shall I call you blind?", it is in a quite different tone that suggests that now he understands why the man chose not to live. The wife had always held the whip, and as "slave" he was willing to bear it for love, but without love life for him had no point. It was not her unfaithfulness so much as her hate that destroyed him. It may be that in this poem Robinson has, as he said himself, "given the reader too much to carry." But the poetry is not in the puzzle. The taut three-stress line, the tight form, and the richness of the first three stanzas save it from failure.

"How Annandale Went Out," a dramatic monologue in sonnet form, is a defense of euthanasia. It is more interesting than many who regard it merely as a puzzle poem realize. Except for the initial confusion caused by the neuter pronoun in the first line ("They called it Annandale") and the "slight kind of engine" in line thirteen, there are no problems of clarity. The "it" is quickly cleared up; the "engine" becomes obvious in the total context. Again Robinson uses a narrator, this time identified as "Liar, physician, hypocrite, and friend," who is attending "it," namely Annandale, his patient. The progressive series of opposed terms *it-him, wreck-him,* and *ruin-man* plays an important part. It gives support to the line "An apparatus not for me to mend," which discloses the patient's hopeless condition; it reveals the narrator's dilemma: as friend and physician he must "find words" (lies) to comfort Annandale; it also explains the physician's hypocrisy and justifies his action. Resolution and clarification come in the sestet:

> I knew the ruin as I knew the man;
> So put the two together, if you can,
> Remembering the worst you know of me.

The worst we know of the narrator is that he is a hypocrite. As a physician, he has sworn in the Hippocratic oath to preserve life, not to destroy it. The line "So put the two together, if you can" is ambiguous. At first it sounds as if the narrator is asking the "you" of the poem to put "the ruin" and "the man" together. This is exactly what he himself was unable to do. He is really asking the "you" to put together the situation: the "wreck" of Annandale and the presence of the physician-friend with his "slight kind of engine." In the physician's view, reflected in his use of mechanistic terms, Annandale has lost all his human characteristics except his capacity for suffering ("A wreck, with hell between him and the end"), and it is this which leads the physician to perform the mercy killing. Although the entire poem is enclosed in quotation marks, it is not until the end that the whole picture becomes clear and one realizes that the narrator's words are addressed to a judge or jury to whom he is attempting to justify himself. The "slight kind of engine" is obviously the instrument the physician used to perform his act of mercy, probably a hypodermic needle. Is it too farfetched to suggest that Robinson may have linked in his own mind *Hippocratic, hypocrite,* and *hypodermic?* At any rate, it is the kind of thing in which he took great delight.

In a fascinating article, David Nivison, the poet's grandnephew, makes a convincing case for the identification of the narrator with Annandale. If we "put the two together" that way, he suggests, "we would have in the poem the words of a dead man, a physician, who had been fatally ill, justifying his own act of self-destruction. In this poetic apologia, as perhaps psychologically in life also, physician and 'wreck' are split apart. Suicide becomes merely treatment of a case; he did the reasonable, if socially unapprovable, thing to do." Thus the poem becomes Robinson's dramatic recreation of the death of his brother Dean, who died suddenly in September 1899, apparently, it is thought, by giving himself a lethal dose of morphine. The poet's deep attachment to Dean is well known, and there is little doubt that his brother's death accounts for his concern with, and attitude toward, suicide. The tragedy of Dean's life — and of Herman's as well — also contributed much to Robinson's sympathetic understanding of the suffering and the defeated. In a sense, their lives have been redeemed in the poetry of their brother, who descended for a time into "The Valley of the Shadow" but emerged. Why some endure and others do not is a topic that engaged Robinson all his life. Consider, for example, people like Miniver Cheevy, Richard Cory, and Mr. Flood.

Even though the general idea of "Miniver Cheevy" is clear, the reader who does not know what is meant by the expression "on the town" misses half of the humor and irony of the poem. To be "on the town" means to be supported by the town, a charity case. Miniver, in other words, is the town ne'er-do-well, the town loafer. The poem is built on the ironic contrast between the unheroic Miniver as he is and his dreams of adventure, romance, and art associated with heroic figures of the Trojan War in ancient Greece, King Arthur's knights in the Middle Ages, and the dazzling brilliance and corruption of the Medici in the Renaissance. What a great figure he might have been, Miniver reasons, had he been born at the right time. That he has not succeeded is not his fault; he uses the classic excuse: the world is wrong! But that in all likelihood he would not have achieved much at any time is made clear by the way Robinson handles his material. The sequence of verbs is used with telling effect: *assailed, wept, loved, sighed, dreamed, rested* ("from his labors!"), *mourned, cursed, scorned.* Mainly, what Miniver did was think. Added irony and humor come from Miniver's attempts to apply his "intellect" to his situation:

> Miniver thought, and thought, and thought,
> And thought about it.

Ordinarily two "thoughts" would have been sufficient to make a point; three "thoughts" would have emphasized the idea of real, intense thinking; but the addition of the fourth "thought" changes the tone of the stanza entirely, making it absurd. What all this thinking amounted to is indicated by the continuation of the sequence to its conclusion in the final stanza, where "thinking" is paralleled by "drinking" ("kept on thinking . . . "kept on drinking"). The repetition of "thoughts" creates an impression of circularity, of going round and round, and establishes a link with "and he had reasons" in the first stanza. Miniver escapes from the world of reality into a world of dreams induced by alcohol. To each stanza the short last line with its feminine ending gives an appropriately tipsy rhythm. The name Miniver with its suggestion of the Middle Ages, patchwork royalty, and minuteness, coupled with the diminutive Cheevy, sums up his minimal achievement. The tone of the poem is one of humor, pathos, and sympathetic understanding, but there is a mocking note also that intimates that Miniver's unfortunate situation is not the result of any cosmic flaw.

In April 1897 Robinson, reporting the local news to Harry Smith, wrote "Frank Avery blew his bowels out with a shot-gun. That was hell." By the end of July he had completed, he told Miss Brower, "a nice little thing called Richard Cory. . . . There isn't any idealism in it, but there's lots of something else — humanity, may be. I opine that it will go." It has become one of the most familiar of Robinson's poems. But poems, like people, sometimes suffer from what familiarity so often breeds. This is especially true if the work appears to be fairly simple and uncomplicated. It may be what led Yvor Winters to remark that "In 'Richard Cory' . . . we have a superficially neat portrait of the elegant man of mystery; the poem builds up deliberately to a very cheap surprise ending; but all surprise endings are cheap in poetry, if not, indeed, elsewhere, for poetry is written to be read not once but many times." This remark is itself surprising, for not all surprise endings are cheap, nor does a surprise ending prevent a work from being read with pleasure more than once. The use of surprise is a legitimate device that occurs in all literary forms. The issue is not whether the reader has been surprised but whether the author has so prepared his ground that the ending is a justifiable one, consistent with the total context. Actually, "Richard Cory" has a rich complexity that becomes increasingly rewarding with successive readings.

A wealthy man, admired and envied by those who consider themselves less fortunate than he, unexpectedly commits suicide. Cory's portrait is drawn for us by a representative man in the street, who depicts him as *"imperially* slim," "a gentleman from sole to *crown,"* " richer than a *king."* An individual set apart from ordinary mortals, Cory is, in their opinion, a regal figure in contrast to his admiring subjects, "the people on the pavement." This contrast between Cory and the people, seemingly weighted in

favor of Cory in the first three stanzas, is the key to the poem. Nowhere are we given direct evidence of Cory's real character; we
are given only the comments of the people about him, except for
his last act, which speaks for itself. Ironically, Cory's suicide brings
about a complete reversal of roles in the poem. As Cory is de-
throned the people are correspondingly elevated. The contrast
between the townspeople and Cory is continued in the last stanza.
The people

> worked, and waited for the light,
> And went without the meat, and cursed the bread;

but they went on living. Cory, wealthy as he was, did not live;
instead, he "put a bullet through his head." This occurred "one
calm summer night." Calm, that is, to the people, not to Cory.
Because the people "went without the meat, and cursed the bread,"
it might seem that life was both difficult and meaningless to them.
But difficulty is not to be equated with meaninglessness; in fact,
Robinson is suggesting just the opposite. "Meat" and "bread" carry
biblical overtones that remind us that man does not live by bread
alone. It is "the light" that gives meaning. In opposition to meat
and bread, symbols of physical nourishment and material values,
light suggests a spiritual sustenance of greater value. As such it
clarifies the intent of the poem, for it reveals the inner strength of
the people and the inadequacy of Cory. Belief in the light is the
one thing the people had; it is the one thing Cory lacked. Life for
him was meaningless because he lacked spiritual values; he lived
only on a material level. Once this is realized, the characteristics
attributed to Cory in the first three stanzas take on added significance and become even more ironic: He was "a gentleman from
sole to crown" (appearance and manner); he was "clean favored"
and "slim" (physical appearance); he was "quietly arrayed"
(dress); he was "human when he talked" (manner); he "glittered"
(appearance); he was "rich" (material possessions); he was
"schooled in every grace" (manner). "Glittered" not only empha-
sizes the aura of regality and wealth but also suggests the specious-
ness of Cory. Even his manner is not a manifestation of something
innate but only a characteristic that has been acquired ("admirably
schooled"). All these details are concerned with external qualities

only. The very things that served to give Cory status also reveal the inner emptiness that led him to take his own life.

An old man living alone on the outskirts of Tilbury Town has gone into town to fill his jug with liquor. Returning home, he stops along the road and invites himself to have a drink. He accepts the invitation several times until the bottle is empty, after which presumably he makes his way back to his "forsaken upland hermitage." "Turned down for alcoholic reasons" by *Collier's*, "Mr. Flood's Party," was first published in the *Nation*, November 24, 1920. The origin of the poem goes back twenty-five years to the time when Robinson was working on his prose sketches. Harry de Forest Smith had told him of an interesting character that he knew. "I am going to take a change of air," Robinson wrote Smith, "and write a little thing to be called 'Saturday,' of which you will be indirectly the father, as it is founded on the amiable portrait of one Mr. Hutchings in bed with a pint of rum and a pile of dime novels." Mr. Flood is one of Robinson's original "scattered lives," wonderfully transmuted over the years.

"Mr. Flood's Party" is in some ways much like "Miniver Cheevy" and "Richard Cory." It is a character sketch, a miniature drama with hints and suggestions of the past; its tone is a blend of irony, humor, and pathos. Yet it is, if not more sober, at least more serious, and a finer poem. It is more richly conceived and executed, and it contains two worlds, a world of illusion and a world of reality. A longer poem with a more complex stanza pattern and a heightened use of language, its theme fully informs the poem: it is dramatically represented by Mr. Flood and given emotional and intellectual depth by means of interrelated allusions and images focused on a central symbol. The theme is the transience of life; the central symbol is the jug. Both the theme and the symbolic import of the jug are announced in the line "The bird is on the wing, the poet says," though only the theme, implicit in the image, is immediately apparent. Its relationship to the jug goes back to its source in the *Rubáiyát of Omar Khayyám*:

> Come, fill the Cup, and in the fire of Spring
> Your winter-garment of Repentance fling:
> The Bird of Time has but a little way
> To flutter — and the Bird is on the Wing.

Whether at Naishapur or Babylon,
Whether the Cup with sweet or bitter run,
   The Wine of Life keeps oozing drop by drop,
The Leaves of Life keep falling one by one.

The transience symbols coupled with the eat-drink-and-be-merry philosophy of the *Rubáiyát* prepare the way for Mr. Flood's party but also intensify the poignance and sharpen the irony. In stanza three, the passage referring to "Roland's ghost winding a silent horn" is the richest in the poem, both in language and in suggestion. It serves a multiple function. The likening of Mr. Flood with lifted jug to Roland, the most courageous of Charlemagne's knights, blowing his magic horn presents a vivid picture, made both striking and humorous by the incongruity. At the same time, however, it is a means of adding pathos and dignity to the figure of Mr. Flood, for there are some similarities. By the time that Roland blew his horn the last time, all his friends were dead; like Mr. Flood he reminisced about the past, and his eyes were dim. Moreover, he had fought valiantly and endured to the end, and these attributes of courage and endurance are transferred to Mr. Flood. (The expression "enduring to the end" has a double reference behind it: it calls to mind the words of Jesus when he sent forth his disciples, "He that endureth to the end shall be saved," a statement that Browning said was the theme of his "Childe Roland to the Dark Tower Came." The Roland allusion is even more subtle. The comparison is not to Roland blowing his horn in broad daylight and surrounded by the newly dead, but to the *ghost* of Roland, and the horn he is winding is a "silent horn." Roland, the last to die, is seeking his phantom friends. So is Mr. Flood. Lighted by the harvest moon glinting on the "valiant armor" of Roland-Flood, this is a world of the past, dim and mute. Fusion of figure and scene is complete. "Amid the silver loneliness / Of night" Mr. Flood creates his own illusory world with his jug.

The significance of the jug symbol, foreshadowed by the *Rubáiyát* and Roland references, becomes clear in an extended simile at the mid and focal point of the poem:

Then, as a mother lays her sleeping child
Down tenderly, fearing it may awake,

> He set the jug down slowly at his feet
> With trembling care, knowing that most things break.

The interplay of similarities and dissimilarities in the relationship of *mother:child* and *Mr. Flood:jug* is too delicate and suggestive to be pinned down and spoiled by detailed analysis. Suffice it to say here that in the child the future is contained; in the jug, the past. Memories flood in as Eben drinks, and he lives once more, temporarily secure, among "friends of other days," who "had honored him," opened their doors to him, and welcomed him home. Two moons also keep him company, one real and one illusory. A last drink and the singing of "Auld Lang Syne," with its "auld acquaintance" and "cup o' kindness," and the party is over. And with a shock we and Mr. Flood are back in the harsh world of reality which frames the poem and his present and fleeting life:

> There was not much that was ahead of him,
> And there was nothing in the town below.

The loneliness of an old man, the passing of time; Eben Flood, ebb and flood. There is no comment, and none is needed.

The striking and functional contrast between the rich figurative language of stanza three in "Mr. Flood's Party" and the final unadorned lines suggests something of the range of language found in Robinson's poetry. Too often Robinson's language has been described as "bare," "dry," "sparse." Such terms are not inaccurate to describe one aspect of Robinson's language, possibly the dominant aspect, but they leave out other aspects and give little indication of his expressive use of language. Robinson's vocabulary is large and varied, and he uses it with great flexibility. Though he delighted in words, he was not intoxicated by them. Sensitive to rhythm and sound, he never used words for mere musicality. Many poets, he said, naming Swinburne and Lanier, had "gone altogether too far in trying to make words do the work of tones. . . . music (meaning tone) begins where poetry (meaning language) leaves off." Robinson, as was evident in his criticism of Moody's work, had no use for "poetic diction," archaisms, or hollow rhetoric. There is no surface dazzle in his work. As a poet he wanted to convey his vision of reality honestly; to do so required honest treatment of his medium. There is no dense imagistic base in most of his poems and no lush color, but Robinson's use of imagery and figurative language is nonetheless notable. He knew how moving the simple can be, and how effective are such devices as gradation, contrast, and climax. The pinnacle of a mountain is discernible only as it stands out above the lower peaks, but a single peak need not be high if it rises from a plain. Frequently Robinson's imagery gains prominence in this way, as in the final tercet of "The Clerks" and the last four lines of "The Mill," where language and emotion rise at the climax. At other times the imagery is woven through a poem like an unobtrusive thread against a subdued background. "Eros Turannos" is a good example. A wife tries desperately out of pride and need, and in defiance of community gossip, to maintain a positive image of her husband which she knows is not true; the husband, aware of her conflict, plays a deceptive role both with her and himself. Intertwined images run through the poem suggesting the themes of deception, age, struggle, and decline, all of which are brought together at the end of the poem. Regardless of the opinions of others, "they / That with a god have striven . . . Take what a god has given";

> Though like waves breaking it may be,
> Or like a changed familiar tree,
> Or like a stairway to the sea
>   Where down the blind are driven.

"The Gift of God," which involves illusion, but not conscious deception, in a mother's blurred vision of the extraordinary powers of an ordinary son, is similar to "Eros Turannos" in the way in which the imagery is handled. The son "shines anointed"; "it seems indeed / A sacrilege to call him hers"; "She crowns him with her gratefulness"; and at the end:

>   upward through her dream he fares,
> Half clouded with a crimson fall
> Of roses thrown on marble stairs.

"The Poor Relation" contains a figure so striking and complex that at first it seems to throw the poem off balance. It is a multiple figure that runs through the entire eighth stanza, a simile that merges into a metaphor which contains another simile:

And like a giant harp that hums
On always, and is always blending
The coming of what never comes
With what has past and had an ending,
The City trembles, throbs, and pounds
Outside, and through a thousand sounds
The small intolerable drums
Of Time are like slow drops descending.

It is only when, we understand its relationship to the rest of the poem that we can appreciate the weight it bears. "The Poor Relation," like "Mr. Flood's Party," is a study in loneliness with an underlying theme of transience; the central figure is an unmarried woman, the poor relation. It would be going too far to call her a female Mr. Flood without a bottle, but the parallels are so strong that one must regard the two poems as complementary. "The Poor Relation," however, was written first. Like Mr. Flood, the woman has lived beyond her time; she has faced and accepted the reality of her situation, she has a ghost and memories, she sings, she has a cage-hermitage, and she hears, not the bird of Time, but the drums of Time. One gathers that in her youth she had been a woman of great beauty and of high social position, for both of which she was envied ("friends who clamored for her place, / And would have scratched her for her face"); that she had been in love with a man who loved her, though their love was never consummated physically ("memories that have no stain"); and that his death marked the end of the fullness of life for her ("Her power of youth so early taken"), her life from that time forth becoming a slow dying. Now she lives alone, receiving a few visitors ("The few left who know where to find her" and who come out of pity, doing "What penance or the past requires"), dependent upon relatives for the "odds and ends" that "she wears and mends." The expository parts of the poem clearly indicate the woman's situation, but the pathos of her situation and the point to which her life has been reduced are embodied in a number of interrelated figures of speech whose significance may not be immediately apparent but which help to clarify both the fused figure in the eighth stanza and the intent of the poem as a whole.

The immediate sense of the two lines that open the second stanza is so clear that one is apt to pass over them too quickly:

> Beneath her beauty, blanched with pain,
> And wistful yet for being cheated.

To think of "blanched" only in terms of a color change, "whitened," is to miss the metaphor. Blanching is a process in which the skin is removed by scalding, as in blanching almonds, a process suggested by "blanched *with pain*." The woman, then, has retained the beauty of her features, but her suffering has left her complexion white (lifeless) and "wistful yet for being cheated." In what sense has her beauty been cheated? The implications of two simple words, "roses" and "grass," both metaphors in the context of the next stanza, answer the question:

> And she may smile when they remind her,
> As heretofore, of what they know
> Of roses that are still to blow
> By ways where not so much as grass
> Remains of what she sees behind her.

What the visitors are trying to do is to cheer her up by inane conversation about how beautiful she still is and that any day now the right man will come along. What is in the back of their minds (and hers) is her unmarried and childless state. "Roses" suggests the beauty and bloom of youth. But her beauty has been "blanched;" she has lost her roses, has, in a sense, been deflowered. "Of roses that are still to *blow*." "Blow," not just "bloom," carries with it a strong generative sense, the promise of bearing fruit, something which for her is impossible now (the idea of barrenness is suggested by "not so much as grass"), and has been impossible, psychologically at any rate, ever since the death of the man she loved ("Her power of youth so early taken"). Though her "memories . . . have no stain," the sexual overtones of these references clearly indicate the frustration of the woman, who has been "cheated" of her natural fulfillment as wife and mother. She has not only been cheated, she has also been crippled:

> None live who need fear anything
> From her, whose losses are their pleasure;
> The plover with a wounded wing
> Stays not the flight that others measure.

Like a bird, "Her memories go *foraging*" ("where not so much as grass / Remains") "For *bits* of childhood song they treasure." In stanza six her "Poor laugh" is described as "more slender than her song." From the bits of nourishment that she is able to forage, one can safely conclude that she herself is also slender. The bird imagery concludes the poem:

> Unsought, unthought-of, and unheard,
> She sings and watches like a bird,
> Safe in a comfortable cage
> From which there will be no more flying.

There she sits in her room, self-imprisoned and alone, looking out at the city (counting "her chimneys and her spires"), her life made up of memories ("bits of childhood song" and a "truant ghost") and a few visitors who drop in occasionally with "odds and ends" and crumbs of pity. Outside, the "giant harp . . . hums / On always. . . ." This complex figure, one can now see, represents not only the contrast between the vibrant and animated world outside, life with its unceasing continuity, and her own almost lifeless state, but from beginning to end symbolizes the movement of her whole life. She, too, was once in harmony with the full rhythm of life, but the continuity was broken, the rhythm fragmented, until now there are only "The small intolerable drums / Of Time . . . like slow drops descending."

"Luke Havergal" is so striking both in imagery and in music that it demands comment. The interesting thing about the poem, aside from its beauty of music and mood, is that it is so uncharacteristic in style and yet so consonant with the rest of Robinson's work. Ever since its publication it has been greatly admired. Allen Tate has referred to it as "a poem in which the hard images glow with a fierce intensity of light, . . . one of the great lyrics of modern times." But there has been widespread disagreement about its meaning. Normally when sensitive readers disagree so thoroughly about the "meaning" of a poem, we should be strongly inclined to say that the poem is a failure. The admiration for "Luke Havergal" is justly based on what the poem does achieve; the disagreements arise out of attempts to go beyond its intention. "Luke Havergal" is a Symbolist poem, and by its very nature is intended to be suggestive. Music, mood, feeling, mysticism — these are qualities that the

Symbolist poet sought. "To fix the last fine shade, the quintessence of things; to fix it fleetingly; to be a disembodied voice, and yet the voice of a human soul": thus Arthur Symons described, in an essay that Robinson read, both the ideal and the achievement of Paul Verlaine, Symbolist poet *par excellence*. Robinson was both aware of and interested in the Symbolist movement, though he had conflicting attitudes toward it. It was Robinson's original intent to include in his first book a group of "Tavern Songs." He was going to try, he said in October 1894, "to put a little mysticism in them, and make them worth while as literature; at the same time trying to make them musical enough to be songs first and poems after." "Luke Havergal," completed by December 1895, was originally part of the Tavern section. Earlier that year Max Nordau's *Degeneration* had been published, a virulent attack on the whole Decadent movement, including Symbolism. In discussing this movement, Nordau not only dealt with the intentions of the Symbolist poets but also described in detail their characteristics and methods, with specific examples. *Degeneration* could easily be used as a primer for the writing of a Symbolist poem. And that is exactly what Robinson did. We can now understand what he meant in his often quoted but unexplained statement that he had written "a piece of deliberate degeneration called 'Luke Havergal.' " It is noteworthy that Robinson dramatized the "disembodied voice" as a projection of a tormented mind. Thus we have, in words of haunting beauty, Luke Havergal, another Tilbury character, done in Symbolist style.

Several other instances of Symbolist poems occur in Robinson's work, most of them done in 1895–1896, though one at least dates as late as 1900. "A Poem for Max Nordau," printed only in *The Torrent and The Night Before,* is a parody of Symbolist techniques, in which Robinson pushed to extremes the "predilection for refrain" and "echolalia" that Nordau noted as characteristics of "degeneracy." The first stanza is sufficient to give the flavor of the whole:

> Dun shades quiver down the lone long fallow,
> And the scared night shudders at the brown owl's cry;
> The bleak reeds rattle as the winds whirl by,
> The frayed leaves flutter through the clumped shrubs callow.

"The Dead Village" and "The Wilderness," at opposite poles in form and rhythm, are both essentially Symbolist in nature. Next to "Luke Havergal," the best of the poems done in this manner is "The Pity of the Leaves," first published in *The Critic*, November 21, 1896:

> Vengeful across the cold November moors,
> Loud with ancestral shame there came the bleak
> Sad wind that shrieked, and answered with a shriek,
> Reverberant through lonely corridors.
> The old man heard it; and he heard, perforce,
> Words out of lips that were no more to speak —
> Words of the past that shook the old man's cheek
> Like dead, remembered footsteps on old floors.
>
> And then there were the leaves that plagued him so!
> The brown, thin leaves that on the stones outside
> Skipped with a freezing whisper. Now and then
> They stopped, and stayed there — just to let him know
> How dead they were; but if the old man cried,
> They fluttered off like withered souls of men.

Several years later Robinson was still occasionally working in the Symbolist vein. In June 1900 he wrote to Edith Brower that he was composing "a symbolical *Twilight Song*"; it was published in *Captain Craig*. Some of the jocose sections of "Captain Craig" contain parodies of Symbolism. But much as he may have been fascinated by this type of poetry, Robinson knew by this time that it was not to be his mode. On September 14, 1900, he wrote to Josephine Preston Peabody," I have come to learn that vagueness is literary damnation (nothing less); and I have determined that whatever I do in the future — excepting now and then an excursion into symbolism, which I cannot wholly throw off — will be tolerably intelligible."

In general, Robinson's use of imagery and figurative language is highly selective and functional. He does not paint with a broad brush, nor is his palette highly colorful. Subtle tonal values prevail rather than striking contrasts. Nature, when it appears, is usually in the background; there is relatively little nature description solely for its own sake. Robinson could, however, render vividly the look and feel of nature. In "The Torrent," for example, he catches in a few lines the movement, sound, and color of "a torrent falling in a glen":

> Where the sun's light shone silvered and leaf-split;
> The boom, the foam, and the mad flash of it
> All made a magic symphony.

The delightful "Isaac and Archibald," one of Robinson's most heart-warming poems, is filled with "the warmth and wonder of the land" and "the wayside flash of leaves" on a hot autumn day. In "The Sheaves" the change of wheat from green to gold suggests the ineffable mystery underlying nature's cycles:

> Where long the shadows of the wind had rolled,
> Green wheat was yielding to the change assigned;
> And as by some vast magic undivined
> The world was turning slowly into gold.
>
> .   .   .   .
>
> A thousand golden sheaves were lying there,
> Shining and still, but not for long to stay —
> As if a thousand girls with golden hair
> Might rise from where they slept and go away.

Occasionally, as in "The Dark Hills," written shortly after the close of World War I, a natural scene informs a whole poem in which image, sound, and sense are indissolubly fused:

> Dark hills at evening in the west,
> Where sunset hovers like a sound
> Of golden horns that sang to rest
> Old bones of warriors under ground,
> Far now from all the bannered ways
> Where flash the legions of the sun,
> You fade — as if the last of days
> Were fading, and all wars were done.

". . . I am what I am," Robinson wrote Mrs. Richards in 1902; "and therefore I have my own paint-pots to dabble with. Blacks and grays and browns and blues for the most part — but also a trick, I hope, of letting the white come through in places." It comes through in his "light" symbolism. "Light," with its counterpart "dark," occurs in one form or another more than five hundred times in his work. This "light-dark" symbolism demands a special word of explanation, for it is dominant throughout his poetry, and it carries the burden of his idealism and the theme of self-knowledge. Because of the simple opposition involved, one may be misled into thinking of it as a simple and static figure. As Robinson uses it, however, it is a highly flexible one with numerous variations. The basic opposition is of course a positive-negative, spiritual-material one, "light" representing, in its broadest sense, wisdom, and "dark" representing ignorance. In its highest sense, "Light" has a cosmic signification; it is identified with the Word, the Logos, as in the opening chapter of the Gospel According to Saint John, where Word-God-life-light are linked to express the eternal creative and unifying principle of the universe. Words like "sun," "dawn," "rays," "shafts," and, in the Arthurian poems, "Grail" and "Vision" form a cluster of substitute symbols for "Light" in this sense. But the "light-dark" imagery also symbolizes the varying conditions of mankind. Each person has his own "light," and he must be guided by it if his life is to be meaningful. This "light" has its source in the Eternal Light, but since each individual is unique his "light" will be correspondingly different from that of others. But in order to follow his "light," a person must know what it is; to do this he must know himself. Self-knowledge is the key to right living, and self-knowledge is attained only by insight. Hence the importance Robinson gives to the verb "to see" in its metaphorical sense of "to understand." But we do not always see clearly, nor do we always act in accordance with our judgment and vision. Imperfection and fallibility are inevitable attributes of humanity. Wisdom is never completely attained; self-knowledge is always partial. Insight comes in "flashes"; we get "glimmers" of "the light" from time to time; sometimes we "consecrate the flicker, not the flame." The spiritual condition of each person is a function of his clarity of vision, and clarity of vision may vary over a wide range with time, place, and circumstance. This range is reflected in the variations of Robinson's "light-dark" symbolism. Instead of just "light" or "dark" as absolutes, there is a spectrum with "light" at one end and "dark" at the other, with gradations in between, viz., wisdom-insight: *light, bright, sight, shine, flash, gleam, glimmer, glimpse, dim, flicker, shadows (clouds), dull, gloom, night, dark:* blindness-ignorance. In Robinson's poetry there are no stereotypes of virtue and evil but individual men and women, children in this spiritual kindergarten, struggling under more or less difficult circumstances and torn by mixed desires and ambitions, to find and follow "the light" that is their earnest of the ineffable Light that darkness can never quench. "I am not one / Who must have everything," Isolt of Brittany says,

> yet I must have
> My dreams if I must live, for they are mine.
> Wisdom is not one word and then another,
> Till words are like dry leaves under a tree;
> Wisdom is like a dawn that comes up slowly
> Out of an unknown ocean.

In addition to short poems of the kind we have been discussing and long narrative poems such as "Captain Craig" and *Tristram,* Robinson wrote a number of poems of medium length that share characteristics of both the shorter poems and the longer ones. His interest in this type of poem, evident from the first, increased as the years went by. Beginning with "The Night Before" in his first volume, he added "Isaac and Archibald," "Aunt Imogen," and "The Book of Annandale" in *Captain Craig;* "An Island" (about Napoleon) in *The Town Down the River;* "Ben Jonson Entertains a Man from Stratford" and the title poem in *The Man Against the Sky;* "On the Way" (Alexander Hamilton and Aaron Burr), "John Brown," "Tasker Norcross," "Rahel to Varnhagen," "Lazarus," and the title poem (about St. Paul) in *The Three Taverns;* "Rembrandt to Rembrandt"; "Genevieve and Alexander," "Demos and Dionysius," and the title poem in *Dionysius in Doubt;* "Sisera," "Toussaint L'Ouverture," "Ponce de Leon," and the title poem in *Nicodemus;* and a few others. Most of these are monologues, several are straight narratives, and a few are dialogues. Character revelation is central, though a number of them are concerned in varying degrees with questions of politics, religion, and philosophy. It is apparent that as Robinson grew older he felt the short poems to be inadequate for the expression of his wider range of interests and play of thought. Though in general the short poems make up Robinson's best work, a number of these medium-length poems must be ranked among the finest things he ever did; some of them also must be counted among the worst. One can see at a glance from the titles that there is greater diversity of subject among these poems. Many of them deal with historical personages, predominantly political and religious figures, rather than with creatures of his own imagination. Why this shift should have occurred is a matter of conjecture. Several factors probably played a part: though he was not isolated from people, he was farther removed from the people and experiences that gave such vitality to his earlier work; his expanding circle of friends certainly widened his areas of interest, not only in literature but also in music, drama, and the arts, as well as in history, politics, and business; he may have felt that he had exhausted his earlier vein or that he was being typed as a poet of a particular genre, or just as a matter of creative growth he may have wanted to try his hand at new things. The whole area of the influence of Robinson's friends of his later years — the Ledoux, the Isaacses, the Perrys, and others — needs further investigation. In any event, when Robinson had a poem in him, as he so often said, it had to come out. Writing to Thomas Sergeant Perry to thank him for a book on the life of Alexander Hamilton, Robinson said that he was also reading James Parton's *Life and Times of Benjamin Franklin* (Franklin was Perry's great-great-grandfather), and then he added: "Fate seems to be driving me back to the days before the Constitution, and I may have to tackle some of the luminaries of the time. I have realized for years that those years present an almost wholly unworked field, but I have wondered also if they are not still a bit too new for poetic treatment. Somehow Lincoln is different, for he seems to be as old as Mt. Ararat and to have bits of the Ark clinging to his clothes."

In an interview with Karl Schriftgiesser, Robinson described something of his method and purpose in writing some of these poems. Schriftgiesser reported that "In writing such a poem he confessed that something more than poetic inspiration was necessary. As in writing a play, there had to be a method, but this I gathered consists mainly in what he called 'brushing up on my reading, doing more or less research.' " Regarding such a poem as "Ponce de Leon," Robinson said "he was trying to see the man himself, rather than the rich and exciting period in which he lived." Sometimes a current biography would stimulate him to write about a particular figure, as was the case with Percy Waxman's *The Black Napoleon,* which led to the poem "Toussaint L'Ouverture," and Ellen Key's *Rahel Varnhagen,* which provided the basis for "Rahel to Varnhagen." The books, however, provided only the stimulus; the interpretation was the poet's own. Esther Bates has said about "Rahel to Varnhagen," which Robinson called "an interpretive monologue," that "he said he did not take his character from Ellen Key's book, . . . he 'precipitated his own characters.' " Some of his "precipitations" are more successful than others. Rahel is one of the less successful. This is due in part to historical factors and in part to Robinson's treatment. It is doubtful that one reader in a thousand has any interest in or knowledge of the brilliant and emotional nineteenth-century Jewess who is the central character in the poem, and the facts that Robinson gives in his note to the poem and in the poem are not very helpful, though accurate historically. The action of the poem takes place five years before her marriage in 1814, though the reader is not told this; nor does there seem to be any great significance in it. Clearly Robinson was not interested in Rahel, in the poem at least, as an historical figure, but in the psychology of a woman who married a man fourteen years her junior. And this is where the interest lies for the reader, but Robinson's treatment is so oblique that one is apt to miss the point. The poem deals with a moment of revelation. At first it seems as if Robinson were merely revealing Rahel's mind as she attempts at first to discourage Varnhagen in his love for her, then comes to accept it. But what Robinson is doing at the same time, ever so subtly, is revealing through Rahel herself Varnhagen's understanding of her mind and heart and her gradual understanding of his understanding of her, that though she has had two previous love affairs that she can never forget, there is still room and need in her for new love. Robinson's approach here is so indirect that Henry James himself would have envied it.

"On the Way" is a dramatic dialogue between Alexander Hamilton and Aaron Burr that is imagined to have occurred in 1794. Interesting in conception, it fails to come off because Robinson attempted to do too much, or rather because he did not bring into relationship the major subjects of the poem. Riding along together on the way to their respective destinations, Hamilton and Burr are forced to stand aside to let President Washington pass. This incident becomes the basis for the conversation that makes up the poem. The first subject is George Washington, whom Hamilton admires and Burr envies. The discussion about Washington leads to further debate about politics and government, in which Burr's desire for position is thinly veiled in his attempts to arouse in Hamilton a feeling that he himself should have had greater eminence. The conversation ends when their roads diverge. The journey together, the verbal duel, and the parting of the ways are symbolic. The implication of the poem is that already in 1794, Hamilton and Burr were "on the way" toward the duel ten years later that resulted in Hamilton's death and Burr's disgrace. Robinson's use of an explanatory note at the beginning of the poem perhaps indicates his awareness that the poem is not clearly articulated as it stands. Though Robinson was undoubtedly intellectually sincere in the poem, one senses a lack of emotional commitment except in the lines about Washington.

With "Rembrandt to Rembrandt," "John Brown," and "The Three Taverns" the case is different. These are moving and convincing poems in which the characters are fully realized. Different as individuals, they possess common qualities of dynamism and dedication; they are all characters who must follow the dictates of their own nature. In these poems Robinson has given us three studies in integrity: the integrity of the artist, the reformer, and the evangelist. They are all monologues uttered at crucial moments. Of the three, "Rembrandt to Rembrandt" is the finest. Robinson presents the great artist seated before a mirror having just completed a portrait of himself; the monologue is Rembrandt's verbal self-portrait of the artist in 1645, three years after the death of Saskia, his wife, and the completion of "The Night Watch" that broke so sharply with the conventions of Dutch group portraits and marked the turn from effects of external brilliance to a world of inner vision portrayed in golden light and shadow. His wife gone, himself fallen from public favor, Rembrandt realistically assesses his situation. He sees only too clearly the difficulty and ignominy of what lies ahead; he knows, too, how easily it could be averted by courting public taste. But that would be at the sacrifice of himself and his art; for he sees himself as "a living instrument / Played on by powers that are invisible," as

> One of the few that are so fortunate
> As to be told their task and to be given
> A skill to do it with a tool too keen
> For timid safety . . .

and he knows "That in Apollo's house there are no clocks / Or calendars. . . ." The blank verse is firm yet appropriately supple as it moves with Rembrandt's shifting thoughts and emotions. It is a magnificent poem. Next to "The Man Against the Sky," Robinson thought that "Rembrandt to Rembrandt" was perhaps the best thing he ever did. One can be sure that in Rembrandt's conception of the artist we also have Robinson's.

"The Three Taverns," "Lazarus," and "Nicodemus" are an interesting group of poems based on the New Testament. "The Three Taverns", a poem of great intensity, is a closely reasoned statement of St. Paul's position interwoven with a theme of the conflict between man-made law and the higher law within. "Lazarus" is an imaginative and dramatic re-creation of what happened immediately after Lazarus has been raised from the dead. As Mary and Martha talk with Lazarus, all three gradually become aware that Lazarus' death and resurrection was Christ's means of foreshadowing the Crucifixion and making them understand its significance. "Nicodemus," like "The Three Taverns," is also strongly concerned with the conflict between the law and the spirit. In a scene paralleling his visit to Christ, Nicodemus, under the cloak of darkness and disguise, visits Caiaphas, the Jewish high priest, in a vain attempt to convince him of the divinity of Christ and that "There is no life in those old laws of ours." Caiaphas, to whom "The laws that were our father's laws are right," shrewdly senses that though Nicodemus may be inwardly convinced, he and Jesus "Will not be seen as man and man together / Where there is daylight in Jerusalem." Robinson's thorough knowledge of the Bible is evident not only in these poems but in much of his work. Though he had no interest in doctrinal distinctions and thought that the Christian churches had failed, he nonetheless found in the Bible a source of inspiration, both poetic and spiritual, and a still viable symbolism of universal application.

"Ben Jonson Entertains a Man from Stratford" is in a class by itself. Though Robinson may have owed something to Taine's *History of English Literature* for the basic conception of Shakespeare's personality, the liveliness of scene and language and the portrait of Shakespeare that emerges are unmistakably and inimitably Robinson's own. Form, point of view, setting, and time conjoin to form a perfect means and vantage point. The poem is a dramatic monologue in flexible blank verse; the speaker is Ben Jonson, Shakespeare's friend and rival playwright, talking to a visiting alderman from Shakespeare's home town; the place is a London pub; the time is 1609, toward the end of Shakespeare's tragic period and before the plays of greater serenity and his retirement in 1611 to his home, New Place, the second largest house in Stratford. As the conversation goes on in language ranging from colloquial casualness and humor to grave eloquence, and filled with subtle echoes from Shakespeare's plays and sonnets, we catch glimpses of the poet-dramatist at various stages in his life, from his boyhood as "a most uncommon urchin,"

> Discovering a world with his man's eyes,
> Quite as another lad might see some finches,
> If he looked hard and had an eye for nature,

to the "poised young faun / From Warwickshire" in his early London days, to the Shakespeare of 1609, "Trim, rather spruce, and quite the gentleman." We see, too, something of the world of the London theater and his fellow dramatists' admiration and envy of one who breaks all the rules and yet succeeds:

> who alone of us
> Will put an ass's head in Fairyland
> As he would add a shilling to more shillings,
> All most harmonious, — and out of his
> Miraculous inviolable increase
> Fills Ilion, Rome, or any town you like
> Of olden time with timeless Englishmen.

But mainly we get an insight into Shakespeare the man and Jonson's love and human concern for him. Jonson fears

> He'll break out some day like a keg of ale
> With too much independent frenzy in it;
> And all for cellaring what he knows won't keep,
> And what he'd best forget — but that he can't.

However, Jonson has a feeling, too, that though "To-day the clouds are with him,"

> He'll out of 'em enough to shake the tree
> Of life itself and bring down fruit unheard-of,
> And, throwing in the bruised and whole together,
> Prepare a wine to make us drunk with wonder:
> And if he live, there'll be a sunset spell
> Thrown over him as over a glassed lake
> That yesterday was all a black wild water.

Running through the whole is the humorously ironic picture of the "king of men" and king of dramatists, disdainful of contemporary praise and future reputation, saving his shillings to become an English country gentleman in "that House in Stratford!"

Of these medium-length poems, two of the finest are also the earliest: "Aunt Imogen" and "Isaac and Archibald," both of which have their source in personal experiences. In both Robinson portrays a warm and delightful relationship between children and older people. The appeal in both is equally the result of Robinson's keen insight into human nature and a seeming artlessness that hardly betrays his narrative skill.

Robinson wrote thirteen long narrative poems, twelve of them after 1916. With the exception of "Captain Craig" (1902), they were published as separate books, ranging in length from sixty-five pages (*Avon's Harvest*) to more than two hundred (*Tristram*). They are all written in blank verse, and, with the exception of the

Arthurian trilogy, they have contemporary settings and deal with problems of people in modern society. They are not, however, merely topical. All of them involve personal relationships of various kinds and complexity. A number of them are concerned with marital relationships (*Roman Bartholow, Cavender's House, Matthias at the Door, Talifer*). *King Jasper* deals with larger social and economic issues. Most of these poems have several characteristics in common. The settings are similar and have few descriptive details. Most of the stories take place in a family home, usually in the countryside; a few trees, a path, a brook, a cliff, a rock formation, and the like, are all the properties Robinson needs for his stage. Although people come and go and one is occasionally aware that there is a world outside, there is little sense of place except as a somewhat isolated spot where people come together. The few details that form the background usually have additional functions, however. Nature, for example, is used to indicate not only the seasons and passage of time but also as an analogue for states of mind: the leaves are green or gold, the light that filters through the leaves is grey or cool or warm, the sunlight is scattered, there are shadows, it is dark outside and in. Sometimes certain objects are given special significance (the dictionary in *Avon's Harvest*) or are symbolic (in *Matthias at the Door* the rock formation shaped like an Egyptian tomb becomes a metaphorical door; Cavender's house is a symbol of the dark house in which Cavender himself is locked). Most of the poems have few characters and again descriptive details are sparse. Usually these details are not specifically pictorial in any individualized way: a round head, a square face, medium build, red hair, hazel eyes, a large nose. Robinson was much more interested in creating an impression of personality and in revealing states of mind and feeling; hence he gives prominence to certain physical characteristics or mannerisms, and he uses details that are generally pictorial but essentially emotive. In *Roman Bartholow*, for example, Gabrielle's morning entrance is described as follows:

> She spoke, and lingered, while he flushed a little
> As he came forward slowly to the door
> Where she was framed and her dark morning beauty
> Was like an armor for the darts of time

> Where they fell yet for nothing and were lost
> Against the magic of her slenderness.

Her husband, Bartholow, kissed her "cool silk mouth, which made a quick escape." Gabrielle speaks to him at this time "in a purring voice / That had somewhere a muffled hardness in it." In *Matthias at the Door,* Garth "was bent, / As only one of those are who have carried / The weight of more than time. . . . He was alive / More with indifference than with life." In *Talifer,* Dr. Quick comforting Althea with his "warm hands like a father's on her shoulders, . . . fancied he could feel her soul and body / Trembling under a thin shroud / Of summer white." Karen's cool and cruel aloofness toward her husband, Talifer, is presented in this way:

> A saint's face of ivory white,
> So moulded as to be almost unholy
> In its immune perfection, with dark eyes
> Always impassable, and with darker hair
> Never disturbed, awaited him and smiled
> At him, with no surprise, as at a friend
> Who had come yesterday, or every day,
> At the same hour.

In all of these poems, there is little external action: characters go from one room to another, they eat a meal, have a drink, go for a walk. Mostly what they do is talk, facing each other and themselves. They talk to each other and they talk to themselves; sometimes, as in *Avon's Harvest* and *The Man Who Died Twice,* they talk to a sympathetic listener who becomes the narrator. As they talk they observe. And so do we as readers.

The long poems have often been criticized because there is too much talk, and too little action and because they are monotonously alike. There is justification for some of this criticism, particularly in *Roman Bartholow,* where the material is overextended. But there is one reader at any rate who would not want *Tristram* reduced by so much as a single line. Actually, it is at the extremes that Robinson is most vulnerable. Some of the short poems are too laconic and have too much weight to bear; some of the long ones are verbose and have too little weight to bear. One must not assume, however, that where there is talk there is no action. Robinson has stripped the long poems to what is essential for his purposes — a spare but functional set, a few characters, a minimum of external details —so that attention may center in the thoughts and feelings of his characters. And here there is action — in the inner world of consciousness. Usually, in these poems, the story begins at a time of approaching crisis or after a crisis has occurred. The characters are troubled people whose world has gone awry: businessmen, lawyers, artists, scientists, musicians; jealous husbands and misunderstood wives; betrayed friends and betrayed selves. And most of the poem is concerned with their attempts to find out why. Hence all the talk and observation, for in order to do so it is necessary to retrace the course of events that led up to the crisis, to recover not only who did what to whom but to uncover unsuspected hurts, hidden motivations, the many psychological lines that have become tangled. It is necessary, in other words, for the characters to understand each other and themselves. Robinson's concern in the long poems is essentially the same as in the short ones. However, the short poems are of necessity thumbnail sketches. At their best, as in "Eros Turannos," for example, their highly suggestive and concentrated power makes them unmatched in the English language, but they do not permit extensive psychological penetration. In the long poems, using a method similar to that of Henry James, enabling us to see and feel with the characters themselves, Robinson takes us deeper into the minds and hearts of his people. If they are not highly individualized, and to some readers this is a limitation, it is perhaps because Robinson was fundamentally concerned with basic human motivation, which after all is pretty much alike everywhere.

Rather than summarize all the long poems, accounts of which are available elsewhere, it will be both more interesting and more enlightening to consider a few in some detail: "Captain Craig," *The Man Who Died Twice,* and *Tristram.*

"Captain Craig," the earliest of Robinson's long narrative poems, is in some ways the liveliest and most interesting. Robinson described it as "a sort of human development of the octaves" and "a rather particular kind of twentieth century comedy." A conscious attempt to do something new and different, it is the embodiment of Robinson's idealism in objective form. And such a form! By comedy Robinson did not mean merely something funny; he had in mind comedy in the Aristophanic sense. Greek comedy, the song of the village, grew out of the Dionysian revels celebrating the harvest of the grapes. As used by Aristophanes in the *Birds, Frogs,* and *Clouds,* for example, it became a vehicle for satire. Filled with buffoonery and bawdy humor, burlesque and parody, strange and grotesque characters, it pilloried contemporary politics, science, poetry, and philosophy in a mixture of coarse and exalted language. Highly personal, it was also serious, as all great humorous writing is. Robinson had a fine sense of humor, a quality that all of his friends have noted. Daniel Gregory Mason once asked him if he did not think his sense of humor had lengthened his life. "I think," he replied, "my life has lengthened my sense of humor." A vein of humor, clearly evident in poems like "Miniver Cheevy," "Mr. Flood's Party," and "Ben Jonson Entertains a Man from Stratford," runs throughout Robinson's poetry. His humor is not boisterous; it ranges from the chuckle of incongruity to the sharp wit of irony. Robinson often referred to himself as a humorist, and once said to William S. Braithwaite, "Why can't the critics see that the basis of my work is humor?" Nowhere is his humor more evident than in "Captain Craig." Unfortunately, at the time it was published, the critics refused to take it seriously.

Robinson's twentieth-century comedy contains as strange a mixture as any that Aristophanes concocted, and with the same purpose: to say something to the people of his time. "Captain Craig" opens with the "false note" of Tilbury Town and closes with a funereal brass band. In between there is satire of Tilbury Town's hypocrisy and sham, of piety rooted in selfishness; there are parodies of Swinburne and Rossetti; dreams of Christ the carpenter and of Hamlet on Lethe's wharf struggling to root out a weed; revels to propitiate, not Dionysius, but Gambrinus, King of Beer; there is a grotesque sonnet in which the Frogs of Aristophanes appear (and in the background "the crude laugh / Of indigent Priapus"); even the Fates appear as fowls. The characters are the poet-narrator, the fiddler Morgan, the learned Plunket, the poet Killigrew; others referred to are an unknown soldier, a blind optimist who lived "as if she thought / The world and the whole planetary circus / Were a flourish of apple-blossoms," a blind pessimist who "would have this life no fairer thing / Than a certain time for numerous marionettes / To do the Dance of Death," Count Pretzel von Würzburger, the Obscene, who played the piano in a way that turned dreams into nightmares. And in the center, the figure about whom the whole poem revolves, is Captain Craig: pauper, king, clown, philosopher, and "self-reputed humorist at large" — "like Socrates."

In the "Octaves" Robinson expressed his ideas from a subjective point of view. In "Captain Craig" he put them in the mouth of the Captain and provided a narrative framework. Captain Craig both states and exemplifies the theme of being true to oneself through self-knowledge, and its corollary of using one's talents. In contrast to the "false note" of Tilbury Town and its blindness, images of music and light are associated with the Captain. When he speaks, there comes "assurance of his lips, / Like phrases out of some sweet instrument / Man's hand had never fitted." He calls himself "One of Apollo's pensioners . . . An usher in the Palace of the Sun"; he cannot think of anything that he would rather do than be himself "Primevally alive, and have the sun / Shine into me." "There shines / The sun," he remarks:

> Behold it. We go round and round,
> And wisdom comes to us with every whirl
> We count throughout the circuit.

Variations and extensions of the theme are carried by related symbols: the child (with strong Christian overtones), laughter, battles, and the phoenix. The battle imagery is not as incongruous as one would think (the central character is *Captain* Craig), for it suggests the idea that life is a struggle and stresses the importance of courage; it also strengthens the parallel between Captain Craig and Socrates. The narrative framework is not merely a mechanical device to break up what would otherwise become a garrulous monologue, but a functional part of the whole. Characters, episodes, anecdotes, as well as imagery, all play a part. The story is told after the fact by a narrator who was himself a participant in the events described. The action, which takes place over a period of nearly a year, is divided into three parts. Part one is concerned with the introduction of the Captain, his rescue by the narrator and his friends, and their initial reactions to him. The narrator, who asks the meaning of the Captain's "nineteenth-century Nirvana-talk," sees "the truth / Within the jest" of the Captain's remarks; his friends, unconvinced, at first regard Captain Craig as a fraud. The narrator, who has to go away for six or seven months, makes provision for the welfare of the Captain and leaves him in the care of his friends. Part two consists of three letters from Captain Craig, in which he expounds his philosophy and comments on affairs back home. Killigrew, spokesman for the group of friends, also writes the narrator about the Captain. Two things become apparent from Killigrew's letters: that the group's attitude toward Captain Craig has changed and that the pauper-philosopher is not well. Suspecting that the Captain is dying, the narrator returns home. In part three the Captain reads his last will and testament ("To you and your assigns for evermore, / God's universe and yours") and talks about death and immortality. The poem closes with an epilogue in which the narrator recalls the gathering of the group on the evening after the Captain's death and the "large humor" of Captain Craig's funeral:

> men stopped
> And eyed us on that road from time to time,
> And on that road the children followed us;
> And all along that road the Tilbury Band
> Blared indiscreetly the Dead March in Saul.

The funeral scene was suggested, as Robinson wrote Smith, "by the alarming pageant on the day when E. R. Protheroe [a local musician] was 'carried to his final resting place.' " Robinson hoped that "Captain Craig" would make people "a little more sensible in their attitude toward the sentimental of life and death — and, incidentally, of funerals." What Robinson did not, perhaps could not, reveal to Smith was that his brother Dean was a Knight-Templar and that, in Mrs. Nivison's words, "at his funeral the commandery marched in uniform to the 'Dead March' in *Saul*." In addition to Robinson's friend Alfred H. Louis, who was the primary source of the portrait of Captain Craig, Dean too was a part of the composite figure of Craig, which also includes characteristics of the poet himself.

In the epilogue the narrator states the impact that Captain Craig has had on the lives of himself and his friends:

> The ways have scattered for us, and all things
> Have changed; and we have wisdom, I doubt not,
> More fit for the world's work than we had then;
> But neither parted roads nor cent per cent
> May starve quite out the child that lives in us —
> The Child that is the Man, the Mystery,
> The Phoenix of the World.

The metamorphosis in the lives of the group is foreshadowed throughout the poem in the name of their gathering place, The Chrysalis, a variant of the phoenix resurrection-rebirth symbol. The interaction between the group of friends and Captain Craig adds a dynamic quality to the poem; it is also a working out of the theme. Although Captain Craig had a history prior to the events that take place in the poem (he said he once "turned a little furrow" of his own, and he spoke of the days when he had "hounds and credit, and grave friends / To borrow" his "books and set wet glasses on them"), when we meet him he is a pauper, a failure in the world's eyes and in his own as well until he becomes acquainted with the narrator and his friends. The topic of failure and the worth of individual lives, which comes up repeatedly in the poem, is related to the theme of self-knowledge. Self-knowledge involves recognition, acceptance, and action — recognition of one's limitations and assets, acceptance of one's role, and living and acting in accordance with it. Captain Craig is given the Socratic role of helping others to see, and in that single talent resides his justification for living. There is an extra twist to the poem. "Captain Craig" contains a good deal of discussion about poetry, and the narrator himself is a poet. At one point, after the anecdote of Count Pretzel von Würzburger and his unique sonnet, Captain Craig, writing to the narrator, remarks:

> And if you like him,
> Then some time in the future, past a doubt,
> You'll have him in a book, make metres of him, —
> To the great delight of Mr. Killigrew,
> And the grief of all your kinsmen. Christian shame

And self-confuted Orientalism
For the more sagacious of them; vulture-tracks
Of my Promethean bile for the rest of them;
And that will be a joke.

At another point, as part of the will, Captain Craig says:

If I had won
What first I sought [material success], I might have
made you beam
By giving less; but now I make you laugh
By giving more than what had made you beam,
And it is well. No man has ever done
The deed of humor that God promises,
But now and then we know tragedians
Reform, and in denial too divine
For sacrifice, too firm for ecstasy,
Record in letters, or in books they write,
What fragment of God's humor they have caught,
What earnest of its rhythm. . . .

It is part of Robinson's "joke" that the narrator in presenting the story of Captain Craig *has* put all these things into a book. But the narrator is a fictitious poet. If we consider the matter further, we find that the joke has a double twist, for there is another poet, a real one, a failure in the world's eyes at the time, who had one talent, whose general philosophy was idealistic and anti-materialistic, and whose poetic creed, at a time when most other poetry was vapid and empty, included the hope that his work would "possess the power of helping others, which, after all, is about the greatest thing a man, or a book, can do" — whose role, in other words, was strikingly similar to that of Captain Craig. Captain Craig is the prototype of a number of other Robinsonian characters, and one can readily understand why. Robinson's serious joke is "Captain Craig." His twentieth-century comedy is not only an expression of his general philosophy but a dramatization of Robinson's role and an illustration of his poetic creed. Its lack of acceptance was a bitter setback to Robinson, and it almost cost us a major poet.

Upon completing *The Man Who Died Twice,* Robinson wrote Mrs. Richards in July 1922, "I have just emerged from the last of my long poem into the valley of the shadow — where one finds the slough of despond, the bottomless pit, and the jumping off place." Robinson's acquaintance with the "valley of the shadow," as we know, was not limited to Bunyan's *Pilgrim's Progress*. After his own emergence from "the valley," he wrote Hagedorn, in 1912, that he had a poem in mind about

> a Valley of my own which will be very queer, and rather long, and will have a tendency to make people sit up, if it is done as it should be done. It is in the distance now, but I know it is there for I can see it. It will be as cheerful as hell . . . and there will be a foggy sunrise at the end with the fog gradually disappearing from a land of joy and song and grasshoppers.

In December 1918, Robinson's "The Valley of the Shadow" was published, a poem in which he brought together as general types some of the "scattered lives" he had been writing about for years: "the broken . . . the weary . . . the baffled . . . the shamed" and others who for one reason or another find themselves lost, their hopes shattered, their identities gone. Among those in "The Valley of the Shadow"

> There were thirsting heirs of golden sieves that held not wine or
> water,
> And had no names in traffic or more value there than toys:
> There were blighted sons of wonder in the Valley of the Shadow,
> Where they suffered and still wondered why their wonder made
> no noise.

The Man Who Died Twice is about one of the "blighted sons of wonder," Fernando Nash, a musician with more than a spark of genius, whose work would have been

> a torch
> Of sound and fire . . . to flood the world
> With wonder, and overwhelm those drums of death
> To a last silence that should have no death,

had he not, because of impatience, destroyed himself in a life of "lust and drunkenness." The narrator of the story is a former musician who had known Fernando Nash twenty years prior to the opening of the poem, at the time when Nash's creative powers had already made him the envy of lesser musicians. When we first meet Nash, his spiritual crisis is over. Reborn, he is beating the bass drum, not in the Tilbury band, but in the Salvation Army band. The narrator, amazed, seeks him out, and in the course of a number of visits to Nash's "gaunt hall-room" (a replica of Robinson's quarters on West 23rd Street) he hears Nash's story of his death and rebirth. In his early years Nash had mastered his craft, developed an original style, and composed two symphonies. Though these works were superior to the tinklings of others, he knew they were but precursors of the great music, his "Symphony Number Three," that he had within him. But he heard also within him "those drums / Of death" that "would be death to follow." Instead of waiting for his great music to come,

> Blown down by choral horns out of a star
> To quench those drums of death with singing fire
> Unfelt by man before,

he "went wallowing / After that other music."

As Nash's story unfolds, it becomes clear that Robinson's concern is with the psychological conflict between creative and destructive forces. It is this conflict that structures the poem, and through the symbolic process of the poem we become participants in it. The conflict is declared in the opposed phrases "I had it once . . . I could not wait," which, like antiphonal voices, carry the theme as they are reiterated throughout the poem. Symbolic counterparts parallel and reinforce the thematic phrases: daemons and devils, the drums of life and the drums of death and two symphonies. After spending nearly twenty years in a life of dissipation, Nash comes to the realization, at the age of forty-five, that his faith and ambition are gone, that he is spiritually dead. In an excruciatingly painful passage of self-flagellation, Nash verbally excoriates himself for failing himself, failing his art, and failing God, the source of his being and creative power. Unwilling to continue to live

> like a rat in a round well,
> Where he has only time and room to swim
> In a ring until he disappears and drowns,

he resolves to starve himself to death after a final debauch that
lasts three weeks. Back in his room, in bed in a drunken stupor,
Nash experiences an hallucination in which a symphony orchestra
of rats, "more than seventy of them / All dressed in black and
white," plays "the first rat symphony / That human ears had ever
heard," a mocking cacophony that symbolizes the degradation of
Nash and his art:

> And still the music sounded, weird but firm,
> And the more fearful as it forged along
> To a dark and surging climax, which at length
> Broke horribly into coarse and unclean laughter
> That rose above a groaning of the damned;
> And through it all there were those drums of death,
> Which always had been haunting him from childhood.

On the wall, a picture of Bach, symbol of all the Titans of music
in whose company Nash properly belongs, comes alive, in Nash's
fancy, nods slowly and ominously while the orchestra plays, then
becomes once more a picture.

The second symphony, a striking contrast to the rat symphony,
comes with dramatic irony. To Nash, still in bed and a week without food, there comes a sudden clarity, followed by a sense of peace,
then fear culminating in joy as he hears the strains of his "Symphony Number Three." That this is no hallucination is made con-
vincingly clear in the poem. The symphony, a verbal *tour de
force* of great beauty, is presented in four movements, a fact that
Mabel Daniels has noted (Robinson pointed them out for her) and
that Richard Crowder has discussed elsewhere. The liquid-fire
imagery, foreshadowed earlier and suggestive of both the flowing
fusion of sound and of creative power, climaxes the symphony.
The first movement, a "quivering miracle of architecture . . . up-
rising lightly out of chaos," introduces the dominant theme of life
and joy ("Joy, like an infinite wine, was everywhere") and the
counter-theme of death and destruction, led by "A lean and slink-
ing mute with a bassoon" and followed by the "slow, infernal
drums" of death and "A singing horde of demons." The second
movement, a quiet movement in a minor key, is one of regret and
lamentation which "went up slowly to the stars / Carrying all the

sorrow of man with it." The third, "A frantic bacchanale," develops the counter-theme, which is silenced by "avenging trumpets." The finale marks the return of the dominant theme, opening with "a marching hymn" which "Sang of a host returning" (all those formerly "driven from the house of life / To wander in the valley of the shadow" and now freed), and concluding with "that choral golden overflow / Of sound and fire, which he had always heard — / And had not heard before."

Weakened by starvation, Nash, in a futile attempt to get some paper on which to record his great work, collapses in a heap at the foot of the stairs. Later he is rescued. Bereft of his creative power, he nonetheless has the assurance that "he had it — once." Moreover, the experience he has gone through has been a redemptive one. In gratitude for finding himself, he spends the rest of his short life in expiation beating "the drums of life" to the glory of God.

The Man Who Died Twice comes close to meeting the classic demands of tragedy. Since the story is told after the fact, no fear is aroused in anticipation of the downfall, but there is pity at the downfall of such greatness brought about through a tragic flaw in the hero's character, and there is catharsis in Nash's recognition of his fault and his resolute acceptance of the truth about himself. When the narrator, just before Nash's death, attempts to excuse Nash's failure by attributing it to a deterministic universe, Nash "would have none of it. He was to blame, / And it was only right that he should lose / What he had won too late." Moral order is at the center of things, and ultimately Nash's fate was the result of moral choice. This is an important point about Robinson's characters and his view of the universe. Though he recognized and accepted the limitations that heredity and circumstance place on mankind, and though he knew that there are some things beyond the control of man, he also knew that there are some things man himself determines. Necessity is the rim of the wheeling universe, but the hub is freedom.

Nash's symphony, which is the climax of the poem, is notable for more than its verbal felicity. It is a symbolic recapitulation of Nash's life, a metaphor of the poem as a whole, and a moral allegory of life as Robinson perceived it. True to the vision he had

had years before of his "Valley" poem, Robinson did include "a foggy sunrise at the end with the fog disappearing from a land of joy and song. . . ." No grasshoppers! Nonetheless, *The Man Who Died Twice* is undoubtedly the finest of Robinson's long poems with a contemporary setting.

Tristram is the third member of Robinson's Arthurian trilogy. Though published as separate volumes, and with an interval of ten years between the first and last, *Merlin, Lancelot,* and *Tristram* are related poems. In addition to sharing the same legendary materials, they are related thematically in a double way. *Merlin* and *Lancelot* are complementary poems, intended to be read together, in which the medieval myth becomes an analogue of a world gone wrong, with particular reference to World War I. "Arthur and his empire" serve, in Robinson's words, "as an object lesson to prove to coming generations that nothing can stand on a rotten foundation." The vision in *Merlin* of

> a crumbling sky
> Of black and crimson, with a crimson cloud
> That held a far off town of many towers.
> All swayed and shaken, till at last they fell,
> And there was nothing but a crimson cloud
> That crumbled into nothing,

becomes a reality in *Lancelot*. With pointed reference to the war, Robinson said that "The most significant line in the two poems . . . is, perhaps, 'The world has paid enough for Camelot.' "

Even as Robinson was working on *Merlin* and *Lancelot*, as early as 1916, he had in mind the possibility of doing a *Tristram*. *Merlin* and *Lancelot*, aside from their interest as war poems, have an independent interest as love stories, and it is the theme of love that binds the two together with *Tristram* to make a trilogy. Frederic Ives Carpenter sees the trilogy as a progressive description of "three distinct but related types of [romantic] love." It is not necessary to identify these types with Emerson's "Initial, Daemonic, and Celestial Love," to agree with Carpenter's thesis. Throughout the poems Robinson rings the changes on "love," "time," and "peace." Only in *Tristram* is love transcendent over time and is peace attained.

Familiar with various retellings of the Tristram story, Robinson,

like others before him, molded the ancient legend to suit his purposes. He eliminated the love potion to make the story psychologically sound. ("Men and women," he wrote, "can make trouble
enough for themselves in this world without being drugged into
permanent imbecility.") He portrayed King Mark, in the latter
part of the poem, as a sympathetic character, an individual changed
as a result of the tragedy. He raised Isolt of Brittany, barely mentioned in Malory's version, to the stature of a major character, and
in doing so not only complicated the plot and provided a foil for
Isolt of Ireland but also created a moving portrait of great tender-
ness. And he embodied the whole in a form that is both convincing
and aesthetically satisfying. Based largely on a pattern of alterna-
tion and contrast, the drama moves inevitably to its conclusion in a
series of tableaus.

The major episodes are presented on three simple but highly
evocative sets: a castle in Brittany with a window looking north
across the sea, a castle in Cornwall (Tintagel) with a parapet overlooking the sea, a castle in England (Joyous Gard) in an idyllic
setting near the sea — always the sea, and rocks, birds, and a few
ships. The cast is almost perfectly balanced: two kings, King Mark
of Cornwall and King Howel of Brittany; two Isolts, Isolt of Ireland, wife of Mark but in love with Tristram, and Isolt of Brittany,
daughter of Howel and also in love with Tristram; two trusted
retainers, Brangwaine, devoted handmaiden of Isolt of Ireland, and
Gouvernail, loyal servant of Tristram; two villains, Queen Morgan,
jealous of Isolt of Ireland and also in love with Tristram, and
Andred, nephew of Mark and jealous of Tristram. All revolve
about the central figure of Tristram, nephew of Mark, in love with
Isolt of Ireland, later husband of Isolt of Brittany. Not directly involved in the action is Gawaine, Knight of the Round Table, a
messenger of good and bad tidings; and in the background, agents
in the reunion of Tristram and Isolt of Ireland, are Lancelot and
Guinevere, whose illicit love is soon to result in the crumbling of
Arthur's empire.

Tristram contains two interlocking stories, each with its own
Isolt and each with its own dominant image that takes on symbolic
force as the poem progresses. The main story is that of Tristram
and Isolt of Ireland; the secondary story is that of Tristram and

Isolt of Brittany. As the action shifts back and forth between Brittany and England, imagery, theme, and structure become intertwined. As each story is told, one is always aware of the other. The secondary story heightens the dramatic quality of the main story, and the two together intensify the poignance of the poem. The result is a poem of great complexity and richness of texture.

The theme of the main story is the transcendence of love over time. The Isolt of this story is Isolt of Ireland, "the dark Isolt," with "Irish pride" and a "dark young majesty"; she is "Isolt of the dark eyes," "scared violet eyes," "wild frightened violet eyes," with "soft waving blue-black hair." Though their moments together are few and brief, Tristram and the dark Isolt are each the world to the other, and their love is described in passages of singing lyricism such as is found nowhere else in Robinson's poetry. At Joyous Gard, for example, Tristram "suddenly felt all his eloquence / Hushed with her lips":

> Like a wild wine her love
> Went singing through him and all over him;
> And like a warning her warm loveliness
> Told him how far away it would all be
> When it was warm no longer.

And again:

> He saw dark laughter sparkling
> Out of her eyes, but only until her face
> Found his, and on his mouth a moving fire
> Told him why there was death, and what lost song
> Ulysses heard, and would have given his hands
> And friends to follow and to die for.

Suffused with warmth as they are, these images usually carry also overtones of foreboding, constant reminders of impending doom, a note that is struck again and again in the dominant image associated with their love. In the first scene at Tintagel in Cornwall, Tristram leans on the parapet and looks down at the sea:

> Down through the gloom
> He gazed at nothing, save a moving blur
> Where foamed eternally on Cornish rocks
> The moan of Cornish water. . . .

Repeated with variations a dozen or more times, this image of the Cornish sea is the most insistent in the poem. It is in this setting that Tristram and Isolt of Ireland declare their love and seal their doom, and it is here that they meet their death. It is here that Tristram first spurns Queen Morgan, humiliates Andred, and angers King Mark, and the turbulence of the image symbolizes the forces arrayed against Tristram and Isolt: jealousy, hate, and time.

The sense of time, so important in the working out of the theme, is subtly changed as the poem develops, moving from earthly time to the timelessness of eternity. Dominant at the outset and intensified by Tristram's banishment, time merges with timelessness at Joyous Gard, and falls away at the death scene as timelessness takes over. Love transcends time in a twofold sense. The first sense is suggested by Tristram at Joyous Gard: "Time is not life":

> Whatever
> It is that fills life high and full, till fate
> Itself may do no more, it is not time.
> Years are not life.

The second sense is expressed by Isolt a few moments later:

> If life that comes of love is more than death,
> Love must be more than life and death together.

Life is measured not in terms of time but in terms of love. It is love that makes life meaningful, and in this sense love transcends earthly time. But since love is spiritual it is also eternal, and in this sense transcends death, the end of time. The transcendent nature of love in the first sense is symbolically reflected, and the second sense foreshadowed, in the episode at Joyous Gard. It is here, in the short span of a single summer, that Tristram and Isolt in the fullness of their love really live, a whole lifetime compressed into a few months. Temporarily isolated at Joyous Gard from the rest of the world, they also live, in a sense, out of time and space, a prelude to their final scene together. At the death scene, back at Tintagel, the turbulent Cornish sea, symbol of all the forces of time and life, is stilled:

> "No sea was ever so still as this before,"
> Gouvernail said, at last. . . .
>
> . . . .

> "No," Mark answered,
> "Nothing was ever so still as this before. . . .
> She said it was like something after life,
> And it was not like death. She may have meant
> To say to me it was like this; and this
> Is peace."

Only a symbolic ship moves, growing smaller and smaller in the distance as it fades into eternity.

The story of Tristram and Isolt of Brittany both frames and divides the main story. Different in tone and color, it is nonetheless functionally related to it, and it gives an extra dimension to the poem. Isolt of Brittany, like the dark Isolt only in name and in her love for Tristram, is otherwise a sharp contrast to her. She is "Isolt of the white hands," "small still hands"; she has a "patient face" like "some white / And foreign flower," with "calm gray eyes" and "gold hair / That is not gold." Though Tristram is keenly aware of "The still white fire of her necessity" for him, his feeling toward her, unlike the "wild wine" of his love for Isolt of Ireland, is one of gentle affection born of "sorrow's witchcraft" that

> Made pity out of sorrow, and of pity
> Made the pale wine of love that is not love,
> Yet steals from love a name.

The contrast between the two Isolts is reinforced and extended in the dominant image of the sea associated with Brittany and Isolt of the white hands. In the opening scene of the poem, Isolt of Brittany is looking northward across the sea. She is waiting, as she has waited day after day, for Tristram, with whom she had fallen in love and "who had sailed away / The spring before — saying he would come back, / Although not saying when." What she sees is

> a blank ocean and the same white birds
> Flying, and always flying, and still flying,
> Yet never bringing any news of him.

This image is repeated twice, once at the end of the midsection of the poem, and once at the close of the poem, both times with significant modifications. Always there are the white birds flying, but in each the sea is different. In the first, it is a "blank ocean"; in the second, there is "white sunlight on the sea"; and at the end, in an expanded image of dazzling light and flight, there is "white sunlight flashing on the sea." The progressive changes in imagery are significant. The primary role of Isolt of Brittany is to understand. She opens and closes the poem, and the increase in the intensity of light is an indication of her growth in wisdom through experience. The first image underscores the theme of the emptiness of life without love. The second one, which comes just after Tristram has left her and Brittany, never to return, is a reflection of the change that love has made in her life. The two years that Tristram spent with her in Brittany during his banishment were the happiest of her life. Though she recognized the "pale wine of love" for what it was, she was nonetheless grateful. Moreover she gave to Tristram the fullness of her own undiluted love. When she learns of his death with the dark Isolt at Tintagel, it is she alone who understands the nature and intensity of their love, and she sees it in cosmic terms. The flying birds that at first brought no news of Tristram also play a part, and they are linked to Tristram and the other Isolt. In the last conversation between Tristram and Isolt of Ireland, at the time when the sea was so still, Isolt also used a flying image:

> "I would to God
> That we might fly together away from here,
> Like two birds over the sea," she murmured then,
> And her words sang to him.

To Isolt of Brittany at the end the flying birds constantly bring news of Tristram. "Now, when I cannot sleep, / Thinking of him," she says, "I shall know where he is." The flying birds and the flashing sunlight also bring peace to Isolt of Brittany, the peace of understanding. "Wisdom was never learned at any knees, / Not even a father's," she had said:

> Wisdom is not one word and then another,
> Till words are like dry leaves under a tree;
> Wisdom is like a dawn that comes up slowly
> Out of an unknown ocean.

Both in time and in import, "The Man Against the Sky" is central in Robinson's work. A reflective poem of three hundred lines, it comes at the midpoint of his poetic career. It is a climax to the shorter poems that preceded it and a precursor of the longer poems to follow. Written at the height of Robinson's creative powers, it sums up, in poetic language almost unmatched in American poetry, his mature and profound philosophic position.

Begun in March 1915, it was completed at the MacDowell Colony in July of the same year. It was Monadnock at sunset that provided the basic image of the poem, so brilliantly established in the opening lines:

> Between me and the sunset, like a dome
> Against the glory of a world on fire,
> Now burned a sudden hill,
> Bleak, round, and high, by flame-lit height made higher,
> With nothing on it for the flame to kill
> Save one who moved and was alone up there
> To loom before the chaos and the glare
> As if he were the last god going home
> Unto his last desire.

It was World War I that provided the immediate stimulus to the poem. Upon completing the poem, Robinson wrote to Hagedorn:

> The world has been made what it is by upheavals, whether we like them or not. I've always told you it's a hell of a place. That's why I insist that it must mean something. My July work was a poem on this theme and I call it "The Man Against the Sky."

But the poem is concerned only indirectly with the war itself; nowhere is it specifically mentioned. The terrifying drama being staged on the fields and in the trenches of Europe was only a part of the larger drama of the destiny of man. And it was with this larger drama that Robinson was primarily concerned. With a pertinence unknown to most of his readers, he dedicated the poem to the memory of his friend William E. Butler, who had committed suicide in November 1912.

"The Man Against the Sky" is a poem of denial and of affirmation. To take it as a poetic statement of the meaninglessness of life, as some have done, is not only a distortion of its intent but a reversal of it. Robinson's purpose was, as he wrote to Amy Lowell, "to carry materialism to its logical end and to indicate its futility as an explanation or a justification of existence." The affirmation grows in part out of the denial, the inability to conceive of an accidental and mechanistic universe, but it is also based on the undeniable persistence of man's will to live. Using a flexible form similar to that of "Lycidas," Robinson created a work highly varied in tone and in movement. Predominantly meditative in mood, it ranges from passages of exalted vision to biting scorn. The meter, mainly iambic pentameter interspersed with shorter lines, and the irregular rhyme match the movement of tone and thought.

The opening lines are built on the simple metaphor of man's upward climb over the hill of life to death, but Robinson renders it in a way that is complex and highly suggestive. In the solitary figure on the mountainside silhouetted against the evening sky, he captures the diminutiveness of the individual man in relation to the universe, but at the same time he conveys a sense of grandeur and mystery as the dark figure moves beyond the uttermost reaches of the natural world and the fires of time, homeward returning. The vision of the man against the sky leads the poet to speculate on the various attitudes of men as they face death. These attitudes are a reflection of the individual's philosophy. The two are inseparable: man's attitude toward death is determined by his philosophy of life, and the way he lives is colored by his attitude toward death. Robinson singles out five different types, to each of which he devotes a stanza, then sums them up as follows:

> A vision answering a faith unshaken,
> An easy trust assumed of easy trials,
> A sick negation born of weak denials,
> A crazed abhorrence of an old condition,
> A blind attendance on a brief ambition.

The sequence is doubly significant. It is one of increasing negation, moving from faith to doubt to denial, from firm belief to nullity. Moreover, as the different types are discussed in the poem, it becomes apparent that the sequence is also chronological, though without sharp demarcations of time, and that the decrease in faith is a consequence of man's increasing scientific knowledge of the physical world, culminating in the twentieth-century scientific materialist, who

> may have built, unawed by fiery gules
> That in him no commotion stirred,
> A living reason out of molecules
> Why molecules occurred,

and who "may have seen with his mechanic eyes / A world without a meaning. . . ." Present and past are linked and the theme is underscored by pointed biblical allusions. The story about the man of tested faith closes with a reference to the "three in Dura" who refused to fall down and worship the golden image of Nebuchadnezzar; thrown into the fiery furnace, they were saved by their faith in God. The scientific materialist who, like Nebuchadnezzar, "may have been so great / That satraps would have shivered at his frown," is compared to "Nahum's great grasshoppers . . . Sun-scattered and soon lost." In Nahum's prophecy of the destruction of Nineveh, Robinson saw a parallel to twentieth-century materialism and its consequences in the war.

In the last two stanzas Robinson attacks the underlying negative assumptions of the materialist and advances his own positive ones. The fact that we no longer believe in heaven or hell is no reason, he argues, to conclude that life is meaningless and that death is mere oblivion:

> If, robbed of two fond old enormities [heaven
>   and hell],
> Our being had no onward auguries,
> What then were this great love of ours to say
> For launching other lives to voyage again
> A little farther into time and pain,
> A little faster in a futile chase
> For a kingdom and a power and a Race
> That would have still in sight
> A manifest end of ashes and eternal night?

If we *knew* that "after all that we have lived and thought, / All comes to Nought," there would be no point in living. But we do not know that this is so, and sensory data alone are no explanation of the universe. Both the origin and the destiny of man are unknown and unknowable, but it is more reasonable, Robinson believes, to conclude that the universe is an ordered and purposeful one rather than the reverse. Moreover, man endures, and his continued will to live is itself an affirmation of belief. Man moves from mystery to mystery, with a brief moment of illumination in his passage through time. In "The Man Against the Sky" Robinson was concerned with both the mystery and, as always, the illumination:

> Where was he going, this man against the sky?
> You know not, nor do I.
> But this we know, if we know anything:
> That we may laugh and fight and sing
> And of our transience here make offering
> To an orient Word that will not be erased,
> Or, save in incommunicable gleams
> Too permanent for dreams,
> Be found or known.

6

Achievement and Perspective

If anything is worthy of a man's best and hardest effort, that thing is the utterance of what he believes to be the truth." These words of Robinson to Harry de Forest Smith in 1897 epitomize the poet's attitude toward himself and his work. Integrity, personal and artistic, was Robinson's dominant characteristic. At a time when many American poets were either lost in a desert of arid academicism or had escaped to a soft and cloudy dreamland of pink cotton candy, E. A. Robinson turned directly to the changing world about him for his material, grounding his poems in the unchanging reality of human experience. Using conventional forms for the most part, he developed a strong and flexible style that carried the unmistakable stamp of his personality and of authentic poetry. For forty years, despite a long and painful period of initial neglect, he gave his "best and hardest effort," and thereby enriched our growing heritage and gained an enduring place among the few other major poets of American literature.

Born into a period of shifting values, both in society and in literature, Robinson came to maturity just as the transition from the old to the new was being made. To place him, as some have done, at the end of the nineteenth-century tradition is a mistake.

That stream, which welled up initially from the springs of Romanticism, trickled out in the first decade of the twentieth century in the effete gentility of such poets as George Woodberry, Clinton Scollard, and Henry Van Dyke. Nor was Robinson merely a transitional figure. The transitional poet *par excellence* was, ironically, William Vaughn Moody, who seemingly had outstripped all others in the field in the early years of the century. The fluctuating forces at the turn of the century are reflected in the ambivalence of Moody's early work. Unfortunately, in his attempts to revitalize the moribund state of poetry, Moody increasingly followed a direction alien to the general contemporary movement. Robinson, alone in his study in Gardiner, Maine, and later in the garrets of Greenwich Village, went his own way. It was the only way he could go, and in the end his way proved to be the more durable.

Except for a trip to England in 1923, Robinson was not widely traveled. While he was abroad he did not even take the opportunity to visit the continent, though he could have done so. "The process of travel is such a bore to me," he wrote to Rosalind Richards, "that I don't even go so far as to think of seeing Paris or Rome. People are more than places to me." Two months in England was enough. There was something in him, he wrote to Ledoux, "that for practical purposes doesn't transplant." Deeply attached to the United States, he was never chauvinistic, and nowhere is his concern for his country more evident than in his criticism of it. Yet, though New England was in his bones, his outlook was not provincial, even in the poems of Tilbury Town, for he felt himself to be part of the larger, continuing tradition of western culture.

We stated at the outset that we could best approach Robinson in the context of the "new poetry." We can now view him in a larger context that includes the former one. Though Robinson was not a formal innovator, he nonetheless played an important part in what became a diverse movement to bring poetry into consonance with the spirit of modern times. In his reaction against the poetry of the late nineteenth century, he broke sharply with the view that restricted the scope of poetry in subject, language, and form. He rejected the idea that only certain subjects were appropriate for poetry and that there was any such thing as "poetic diction." The function of the poet, he felt, is to deal truthfully with human experience as he sees it. The only limitations derive from the mind and temperament of the poet and the demands of art. The wide play of thought and emotion in Robinson's poetry and his expressive use of language, ranging from the conversational rhythms of ordinary speech to formal patterns of eloquence, are part of his contribution to modern poetry. Though he wrote in conventional forms, he did so with consummate skill, adapting means to ends as only a master artist can. He restored to the sonnet a vigor long lost and extended its range to include the dramatic treatment of character and situation. His use of wit and irony, his intellectuality and objectivity, and his concern with the individual psyche and inner conflict place him in the mainstream of contemporary poetry.

Robinson's most notable achievement lies in his perception and depiction of character. With penetrating psychological insight, he drew a gallery of portraits unequaled in American poetry — Aaron Stark, Richard Cory, Cliff Klingenhagen, Captain Craig, Isaac and Archibald, Aunt Imogen, Miniver Cheevy, Tasker Norcross, Fernando Nash, to mention only a few. In "Ben Jonson Entertains a Man from Stratford" he gave us the liveliest poetic portrait that we have of Will Shakespeare, and in the Arthurian poems he gave us a new Merlin, Lancelot, and Tristram, retaining the universality of the old legends and endowing them with contemporary significance. Cryptic at times and at times verbose, Robinson is at his best in dealing with specific cases, especially in the shorter poems of highly suggestive annd concentrated power like "Eros Turannos" and "Mr. Flood's Party." Like Hawthorne, whom he resembled in his moral concern and in his interest in the hidden caverns of the mind and heart, Robinson composed in light and shade, knowing how mixed the motivations of human behavior are, how difficult it is to know oneself, and how impossible it is to know someone else. He presented his characters with a detachment often ironic and sometimes humorous, without oversimplification and without sentimentality, sometimes with pity but always with sympathy. Robinson's poetic vision was focused on what is essentially human, and it is this vision that is most clearly reflected in his work. At the same time, it mirrors an age of anxiety, an age that has become even more anxious in the generation born since Robinson's death. What he had to say to his own generation applies with even greater force today.

It would be rash to prophesy what Robinson's ultimate position will be. The estimation of literary worth is always relative and never final. Even Shakespeare and Milton have had their ups and downs. Yet if sincerity, a sensitive and penetrating mind, and the ability to express in moving language ideas and feelings of universal significance are criteria, Robinson's position as a poet of the first order seems assured. With the four American poets of the nineteenth century who are generally conceded to be of major importance, he compares more than favorably and in some ways surpassingly well. Poe's slender offering, superb in its limited way, is no match, except in technical brilliance, for the range and profundity of Robinson's work. Emerson, whom Robinson regarded as "the greatest poet who ever wrote in America," was as penetrating as Robinson and had a more seminal mind, but he is inferior to Robinson in technical skill and mastery of form. Whitman, broader in range and at his best master of a different poetic mode, is too uneven and too often diffuse. Emily Dickinson, whose hard and iridescent gems glow with an intensity unmatched even in Robinson's concentrated shorter poems, is more limited, and she suffers, through no fault of her own, because so many of her poems never received the final polish. When we turn to Robinson's contemporaries the list of comparable poets becomes more restricted. Now that the hubbub and excitement of the period has died down, we can see that much of the experimentation, important and necessary as it was, depended more on novelty than originality, and that sensationalism often substituted for true feeling. There was too much papier-mâché and too little bronze. There were of course some fine poets who produced some excellent poems, but of all of those variously regarded as "new poets" — Frost, Sandburg, Masters, Amy Lowell, Fletcher, Lindsay, Williams, Pound, Eliot, and a host of lesser figures — only two appear to be of equal stature with Robinson, namely, Frost and Eliot. Frost took the middle path, as did Robinson, adapting older forms to make modern poems; equally concerned with the human mind and heart, he has a more direct appeal than Robinson, but he is more of a regional poet and less profound. Eliot used his individual talent to fuse two traditions, the English metaphysical and the French symbolist, to make his special brand of "new poetry"; erudite and profound, he is, like Robinson, though from an orthodox position, concerned with questions of moral order in a materialistic world, but he is less accessible because of the esoteric nature of much of his work.

We do not yet have a complete picture of Robinson and his period. We are too close in time to see things in full perspective, and there is still much we do not know. We need to know, first of all, more about Robinson's life. Two biographies and two important volumes of his letters have been published, but the biographies are not definitive and the published letters constitute only a small portion of Robinson's correspondence. Chard Powers Smith's recent "portrait" of E. A. Robinson adds some new factual material, but it also contains much conjecture. The bulk of the letters remain unpublished in the Houghton Memorial Library at Harvard, the Colby College Library, Princeton University Library, the New York Public Library, the Alderman Library at the University of Virginia, and the Library of Congress; some of the letters are still in private hands. These must be published before a definitive biography can be written. Additional information will not add to or detract from the value of Robinson's poetry, but it may help us to understand the man and his work more fully. It may be, too, that when we get a better perspective on the development of American poetry in the first half of the century, we shall see more clearly just how important Robinson's poetry is. Of all of Robinson's friends, it was the one with the greatest potential who placed the highest value on Robinson's work. "When we're all dead and buried," Moody said to Ridgely Torrence, "E. A. will go thundering down the ages."

Selected Bibliography

Robinson's Chief Works

Individual Volumes of Poetry

The Torrent and The Night Before. Cambridge, Mass.: Privately printed, 1896.

The Children of the Night. Boston: Richard G. Badger & Company, 1897.

Captain Craig. Boston and New York: Houghton, Mifflin & Company, 1902.

The Town Down the River. New York: Charles Scribner's Sons, 1910.

The Man Against the Sky. New York: The Macmillan Company, 1916.

Merlin. New York: The Macmillan Company, 1917.

Lancelot. New York: Thomas Seltzer, 1920.

The Three Taverns. New York: The Macmillan Company, 1920.

Avon's Harvest. New York: The Macmillan Company, 1921.

Roman Bartholow. New York: The Macmillan Company, 1923.

The Man Who Died Twice. New York: The Macmillan Company, 1924.

Dionysius in Doubt. New York: The Macmillan Company, 1925.

155

Tristram. New York: The Macmillan Company, 1927.

Sonnets 1889–1927. New York: The Macmillan Company, 1928.

Cavender's House. New York: The Macmillan Company, 1929.

The Glory of the Nightingales. New York: The Macmillan Company, 1930.

Matthias at the Door. New York: The Macmillan Company, 1931.

Nicodemus. New York: The Macmillan Company, 1932.

Talifer. New York: The Macmillan Company, 1933.

Amaranth. New York: The Macmillan Company, 1934.

King Jasper. New York: The Macmillan Company, 1935.

COLLECTIONS OF POEMS

Collected Poems of Edwin Arlington Robinson. New York: The Macmillan Company, 1937.

Edwin Arlington Robinson Poems Selected, With a Preface, by Bliss Perry. New York: The Macmillan Company, 1931.

Selected Early Poems and Letters of E. A. Robinson, edited by Charles T. Davis. New York: Holt, Rinehart, and Winston, 1960.

Selected Poems of Edwin Arlington Robinson, edited by Morton D. Zabel. Introduction by James Dickey. New York: The Macmillan Company, 1965.

Tilbury Town, Selected Poems of Edwin Arlington Robinson. Introduction and Notes by Lawrance Thompson. New York: The Macmillan Company, 1953.

PROSE

Van Zorn, A Comedy in Three Acts. New York: The Macmillan Company, 1914.

The Porcupine, A Drama in Three Acts. New York: The Macmillan Company, 1915.

The Peterborough Idea. Privately printed, 1917.

Selections From the Letters of Thomas Sergeant Perry, edited, with an introduction, by Edwin Arlington Robinson. New York: The Macmillan Company, 1929.

"The First Seven Years," *The Colophon,* December 1930, pp. 71–78. Reprinted in *Breaking Into Print,* Elmer Adler, ed. New York: Simon and Schuster, 1937, pp. 163–70.

LETTERS

Letters to Howard George Schmitt. Edited by Carl J. Weber. Waterville, Maine: Colby College Library, 1943.

Selected Letters of Edwin Arlington Robinson. Introduction by Ridgely Torrence. New York: The Macmillan Company, 1940.

Untriangulated Stars: Letters of Edwin Arlington Robinson to Harry de Forest Smith, 1890–1905. Edited by Denham Sutcliffe. Cambridge, Mass.: Harvard University Press, 1947.

See also:

Fussell, Edwin S. "Robinson to Moody: Ten Unpublished Letters," *American Literature,* XXIII (May 1951), 173–87.

Lowe, Robert Liddell, "Edwin Arlington Robinson to Harriet Monroe: Some Unpublished Letters," *Modern Philology,* LX, 31–40.

———. "A Letter of Edwin Arlington Robinson to James Barstow," *New England Quarterly,* XXXVII (September 1964), 390–92.

———. "Two Letters of Edwin Arlington Robinson. A Note on His Early Reception," *New England Quarterly,* XXVII (June 1954), 257–61.

Mason, Daniel G. "Early Letters of Edwin Arlington Robinson," *Virginia Quarterly Review,* XIII (Winter 1937), 52–69.

———. "Edwin Arlington Robinson, A Group of Letters," *Yale Review,* XXV (Summer 1936), 860–64.

———. "Letters of Edwin Arlington Robinson to Daniel Gregory Mason," *Virginia Quarterly Review,* XIII (Spring 1937), 223–40.

BIBLIOGRAPHY

Hogan, Charles Beecher. *A Bibliography of Edwin Arlington Robinson.* New Haven: Yale University Press, 1936.

———. "Edwin Arlington Robinson: New Bibliographical Notes," *Papers of the Bibliographical Society of America,* XXXV (Quarter II), 115–44.

Lippincott, Lillian. *A Bibliography of the Writings and Criticisms of Edwin Arlington Robinson.* Boston: F. W. Faxon, 1937.

See also:

Adams, Léonie. "The Ledoux Collection of Edwin Arlington Robinson," *Library of Congress Quarterly Journal of Current Acquisitions,* VII (November 1949), 9–13.

Collamore, H. Bacon. *Edwin Arlington Robinson 1869–1935: A Collection of His Works from the Library of Bacon Collamore.* [Most of these items are now part of the Robinson collection at the Colby College Library.]

Isaacs, Edith. "Edwin Arlington Robinson, A Descriptive List of the Lewis M. Isaacs Collection of Robinsoniana," *Bulletin of the New York Public Library*, LII (May 1948), 211–33.

Biography

Hagedorn, Hermann. *Edwin Arlington Robinson*. New York: The Macmillan Company, 1938.

Neff, Emery. *Edwin Arlington Robinson*. New York: William Sloane Associates, Inc., 1948.

Richards, Laura E. *E. A. R.* Cambridge, Mass.: Harvard University Press, 1936.

See also:

Dunbar, Olivia Howard [Mrs. Ridgely Torrence]. *A House in Chicago*. Chicago: The University of Chicago Press, 1947.

Mason, Daniel Gregory. *Music in My Time*. New York: The Macmillan Company, 1938.

Moody, William Vaughn. *Letters to Harriet*. Edited, with Introduction and Conclusion, by Percy MacKaye. Boston and New York: Houghton Mifflin Company, 1935.

Critical and Interpretative Studies

Books and Pamphlets

Barnard, Ellsworth. *Edwin Arlington Robinson, A Critical Study*. New York: The Macmillan Company, 1952.

Bates, Esther. *Edwin Arlington Robinson and His Manuscripts*. Waterville, Maine: Colby College Library, 1944.

Beebe, Lucius. *Aspects of the Poetry of Edwin Arlington Robinson*, with a bibliography by Bradley Fisk. Cambridge, Mass.: The Dunster House Bookshop, 1928.

Bogan, Louise. *Achievement in American Poetry 1900–1950*. Chicago: Henry Regnery Company, 1951, pp. 19–22.

Brooks, Van Wyck. *New England: Indian Summer 1865–1915*. New York: E. P. Dutton & Co., Inc., 1940, pp. 491–99.

Brown, Rollo Walter. *Next Door to a Poet.* New York: D. Appleton-Century Co., 1937.

Cestre, Charles. *An Introduction to Edwin Arlington Robinson.* New York: The Macmillan Company, 1930.

Coffin, Robert P. T. *New Poetry of New England: Robinson and Frost.* Baltimore: Johns Hopkins Press, 1938.

Conner, Frederick William. *Cosmic Optimism.* Gainesville: University of Florida Press, 1949, pp. 365–74.

Coxe, Louis. *E. A. Robinson.* University of Minnesota Pamphlets on American Writers, No. 17. Minneapolis: University of Minnesota Press, 1962.

Fussell, Edwin S. *Edwin Arlington Robinson, The Literary Background of a Traditional Poet.* Berkeley and Los Angeles: University of California Press, 1954.

Gregory, Horace, and Zaturenska, Marya. *A History of American Poetry 1900–1940.* New York: Harcourt, Brace and Company, 1946, pp. 107–32.

Humphry, James, III. *The Library of Edwin Arlington Robinson.* Waterville, Maine: Colby College Press, 1950.

Kaplan, Estelle. *Philosophy in the Poetry of Edwin Arlington Robinson.* New York: Columbia University Press, 1940.

Lowell, Amy. *Tendencies in Modern American Poetry.* Boston and New York: Houghton Mifflin Company, 1917, pp. 3–75.

Morris, Lloyd. *The Poetry of Edwin Arlington Robinson.* New York: The Macmillan Company, 1923.

Pearce, Roy Harvey. *The Continuity of American Poetry.* Princeton, New Jersey: Princeton University Press, 1961, pp. 256–69.

Redman, Ben Ray. *Edwin Arlington Robinson.* New York: Robert M. McBride & Company, 1926.

Smith, Chard Powers. *Where the Light Falls, A Portrait of Edwin Arlington Robinson.* New York: The Macmillan Company, 1965.

Tate, Allen. *On the Limits of Poetry.* New York: Swallow Press, 1948, pp. 358–64.

Untermeyer, Louis. *Edwin Arlington Robinson, A Reappraisal.* Washington: Library of Congress, 1963.

Van Doren, Mark. *Edwin Arlington Robinson.* New York: The Literary Guild of America, 1927.

Williams, Stanley T. "Edwin Arlington Robinson," Chapter 69 in *Literary History of the United States,* edited by Robert E. Spiller *et al.* New York: The Macmillan Company, 1948, pp. 1157–70.

Winters, Yvor. *Edwin Arlington Robinson.* Norfolk, Conn.: New Directions, 1946.

ARTICLES

Adams, Richard P. "The Failure of Edwin Arlington Robinson," *Tulane Studies in English*, XI (1961), 97–151.

Adler, J. H. "Robinson's Gawaine," *English Studies*, XXXIX (February 1958), 1–20.

Aiken, Conrad. "The Poetry of Mr. E. A. Robinson," *Freeman*, IV (September 21, 1921), 43–46.

Allen, James L., Jr. "Symbol and Theme in 'Mr. Flood's Party,' " *Mississippi Quarterly*, XV (Fall 1962), 139–43.

Anderson, Wallace L. "E. A. Robinson's 'Scattered Lives'," *American Literature*, XXXVIII (January 1967), 498–507.

App, Austin J. "Edwin Arlington Robinson's Arthurian Poems," *Thought*, X (December 1935), 468–79.

Boynton, Percy H. "American Authors of Today — Edwin Arlington Robinson," *English Journal*, XI (September 1922), 383–91.

Brown, David. "E. A. Robinson's Later Poems," *New England Quarterly*, X (September 1937), 487–502.

———. "Some Rejected Poems of Edwin Arlington Robinson," *American Literature*, VII (January 1936) 395–414.

Brown, Maurice F. "Moody and Robinson," *Colby Library Quarterly*, Series V, No. 8 (December 1960), 185–94.

Carpenter, Frederic Ives. "Tristram the Transcendent," *New England Quarterly*, XI (September 1938), 501–23.

Cary, Richard. "E. A. Robinson as Soothsayer," *Colby Library Quarterly*, Series VI, No. 6 (June 1963), 233–45.

Cestre, Charles. "Edwin Arlington Robinson, Maker of Myths," *Mark Twain Quarterly*, II (Spring 1938), 3–8.

Childers, W. C. "Edwin Arlington Robinson's Proper Names," *Names*, III (December 1955), 223–29.

Collamore, H. Bacon. "Robinson and the War," *Colby Library Quarterly*, I (March 1943), 30–31.

Colton, Arthur W. "Edwin Arlington Robinson," *Literary Review* [of the *New York Evening Post*], III (June 23, 1923), 781–82.

Coxe, Louis O. "E. A. Robinson: The Lost Tradition," *Sewanee Review*, LXII (Spring 1954), 247–66.

Crowder, Richard. "E. A. Robinson and the Meaning of Life," *Chicago Review*, XV (Summer 1961), 5–17.

———. "E. A. Robinson's Camelot," *College English*, IX (November 1947), 72–79.

Crowder, Richard. "E. A. Robinson's Craftsmanship: Opinions of Contemporary Poets," *Modern Language Notes*, LXI (February 1946), 1–14.

————. "E. A. Robinson's Symphony: *The Man Who Died Twice,*" *College English*, XI (December 1949), 141–44.

————. " 'Here Are the Men. . .': E. A. Robinson's Male Character Types," *New England Quarterly*, XVIII (September 1945), 346–67.

————. "Man Against the Sky," *College English*, XIV (February 1953), 269–76.

————. "Redemption for the Man of Iron," *Personalist*, XLIII, 46–56.

————. "Robinson's *Talifer:* The Figurative Texture," *Boston University Studies in English*, IV (Winter 1960), 214–47.

————. "The Emergence of E. A. Robinson," *South Atlantic Quarterly*, XLV (January 1946), 89–98.

Daniels, Mabel. "Edwin Arlington Robinson: A Musical Memoir," *Colby Library Quarterly*, Series VI, No. 6 (June 1963), 219–33.

————. "Robinson's Interest In Music," *Mark Twain Quarterly*, II (Spring 1938), 15, 24.

Dauner, Louise. "Avon and Cavender: Two Children of the Night," *American Literature*, XIV (March 1942), 55–65.

————. "The Pernicious Rib: E. A. Robinson's Concept of Feminine Character," *American Literature*, XV (May 1943), 139–58.

————. "Vox Clamantis: Edwin Arlington Robinson as a Critic of American Democracy," *New England Quarterly*, XV (September 1942), 401–26.

Davis, Charles T. "Image Patterns in the Poetry of Edwin Arlington Robinson," *College English*, XXII (March 1961), 380–86.

Donaldson, Scott. "The Alien Pity: A Study of Character in E. A. Robinson's Poetry," *American Literature*, XXXVIII (May 1966), 219–29.

Drinkwater, John. "Edwin Arlington Robinson," *Yale Review*, XI (April 1922), 467–76.

DuBois, Arthur E. "The Cosmic Humorist," *Mark Twain Quarterly*, II (Spring 1938), 11–13.

Eby, Cecil D., Jr. "Edwin Arlington Robinson on Higher Education," *Colby Library Quarterly*, Series V, 163–64.

Evans, Nancy. "Edwin Arlington Robinson," *Bookman*, LXXV (November 1932), 675–81.

Fletcher, John Gould. "Portrait of Edwin Arlington Robinson," *North American Review*, CCXLIV (Autumn 1937), 24–26.

Free, William J. "E. A. Robinson's Use of Emerson," *American Literature,* XXXVIII (March 1966), 69–84.

French, Lewis Joseph. "The Younger Poets of New England," *New England Magazine,* XXXIII (December 1905), 425–26.

Gregory, Horace and Zaturenska, Marya. "The Vein of Comedy in E. A. Robinson's Poetry," *American Bookman,* I (Fall 1944), 43–64.

Hertz, Robert N. "Two Voices of the American Village: Robinson and Masters," *Minnesota Review,* II, 345–58.

Hill, Robert W. "More Light on a Shadowy Figure: A. H. Louis, the Original of Edwin Arlington Robinson's 'Captain Craig'," *Bulletin of the New York Public Library,* LX (August 1956), 373–77.

Hudson, H. H. "Robinson and Praed," *Poetry,* LXI (February 1943), 612–20.

Isaacs, Lewis M. "E. A. Robinson Speaks of Music," *New England Quarterly,* XXII (December 1947), 499–510.

Kilmer, Joyce. "A Classic Poet," *New York Times Review of Books,* September 8, 1912, p. 487.

Latham, G. W. "Robinson at Harvard," *Mark Twain Quarterly,* II (Spring 1938), 19–20.

Ledoux, Louis. "Psychologist of New England," *Saturday Review of Literature,* XII (October 19, 1935), 3–4, 16, 18.

Lowell, Amy. "A Bird's Eye View of E. A. Robinson," *Dial,* LXXII (February 1922), 130–42.

MacVeagh, Lincoln. "Edwin Arlington Robinson," *New Republic,* II (April 10, 1915), 267–68.

Maynard, Theodore. "Edwin Arlington Robinson," *Catholic World,* CXLI, 266–75.

Miller, Perry. "The New England Conscience," *American Scholar,* XXVIII (Winter 1958–59), 149–58.

Monroe, Harriet. "Robinson as Man and Poet," *Poetry,* XLVI (June 1953), 150–57.

Moran, Ronald. "Avon's Harvest Re-examined," *Colby Library Quarterly,* Series VI, No. 6 (June 1963), 247–54.

Nivison, David S. "Does It Matter How Annandale Went Out?", *Colby Library Quarterly,* Series V, No. 8 (December 1960), 170–85.

Oliver, Egbert S. "Robinson's Dark-Hill-to-Climb Image," *Literary Criterion* (Mysore), III (Summer 1959), 36–52.

Perrine, Laurence. "Contemporary Reference of Robinson's Arthurian Poems," *Twentieth Century Literature,* VIII, 74–82.

———. "A Reading of 'Miniver Cheevy'," *Colby Library Quarterly,* Series VI, 65–74.

Pipkin, E. Edith. "The Arthur of Edwin Arlington Robinson," *English Journal,* XIX (March 1930), 183–95.

Robbins, Howard Chandler. "The Classicism of Edwin Arlington Robinson," *Congregational Quarterly,* XIV (April 1936), 166–71.

Scott, Winfield Townley. "Great and Austere Poet," *Poetry,* LXX (March 1947), 94–98.

————. "Robinson in Focus," *Poetry,* LXV (January 1945), 209–14.

————. "Robinson to Robinson," *Poetry,* LIV (May 1939), 92–100.

————. "To See Robinson," *New Mexico Quarterly,* XXVI (Summer 1956), 161–78.

————. "Unaccredited Profession," *Poetry,* L (June 1937), 150–54.

Sinclair, May. "Three American Poets of To-day," *Atlantic Monthly,* XCVIII (September 1906), 330–33.

St. Clair, George. "E. A. Robinson and Tilbury Town," *New Mexico Quarterly,* IV (May 1934), 95–107.

————. "Edwin Arlington Robinson on Time," *New Mexico Quarterly,* IX (August 1939), 150–56.

Stevick, Robert Davis. "Robinson and William James," *University of Kansas City Review,* XXV (June 1959), 293–301.

Stovall, Floyd. "The Optimism Behind Robinson's Tragedies," *American Literature,* X (March 1938), 1–23.

Sutcliffe, W. Denham. "The Original of Robinson's Captain Craig," *New England Quarterly,* XVI (September 1943), 407–31.

Theis, O. F. "Edwin Arlington Robinson," *Forum,* LI (February 1914), 305–12.

Torrence, O. H. D. "The Poet at the Breakfast Table," *Colophon,* n.s. III (Winter 1938), 92–99.

Van Norman, C. Elta. "Captain Craig," *College English,* II (February 1941), 462–75.

Waggoner, Hyatt Howe. "E. A. Robinson and the Cosmic Chill," *New England Quarterly,* XIII (March 1940), 65–84. [Reprinted in *The Heel of Elohim,* Norman: University of Oklahoma Press, 1950, pp. 18–40.]

Walsh, W. T. "Some Recollections of E. A. Robinson," *Catholic World,* CLV (August 5, 1942), 703–12.

Wearing, Thomas. "Edwin Arlington Robinson — New England Poet-Philosopher," *Colgate-Rochester Divinity School Bulletin,* XIV (February 1942), 162–74.

Weber, Carl J. "E. A. Robinson's Translation of Sophocles," *New England Quarterly,* XVII (December 1944), 604–05.

Weber, Carl J. "Poet and President," *New England Quarterly,* XVI (December 1943), 615–26.

Weeks, Lewis E. Jr. "E. A. Robinson's Poetics," *Twentieth Century Literature,* XI (October 1965), 131–45.

Williams, A. M. "Edwin Arlington Robinson, Journalist," *New England Quarterly,* XV (December 1942), 715–24.

Winters, Yvor. "Religious and Social Ideas in the Didactic Work of E. A. Robinson," *Arizona Quarterly,* I (Spring 1945), 70–85.

Zabel, Morton D. "Edwin Arlington Robinson," *Commonweal,* XVII (February 15, 1933), 436–38.

————. "Robinson in America," *Poetry,* XLVI (June 1935), 157–62.

————. "Robinson: The Ironic Discipline," *Nation,* CXLV (August 28, 1937), 222–23.

DISSERTATIONS

Ayo, Nicholas. "E. A. Robinson and the Bible." Duke University, 1965.

Betsky, Seymour. "Some Aspects of the Philosophy of Edwin Arlington Robinson: Self-Knowledge, Self-Acceptance, and Conscience." Harvard University, 1942.

Burton, David H. "Christian Conservatism in the Poetry of Edwin Arlington Robinson." Georgetown University, 1953.

Crowder, Richard H. "Three Studies of Edwin Arlington Robinson: His Male Characters, His Emergence, and His Contemporaneous Reputation." State University of Iowa, 1944.

Dauner, Margaret L. "Studies in Edwin Arlington Robinson." State University of Iowa, 1944.

Davis, Charles T. "The Poetic Drama of Moody, Robinson, Torrence, and MacKaye, 1894–1909." New York University, 1951.

Dechert, Peter. "Edwin Arlington Robinson and Alanson Tucker Schumann: A Study in Influences." University of Pennsylvania, 1955.

Durling, Dwight L. "A Critical Account of the Work of Robinson in the Light of Its Position in American Thought and American Literary History." Queens College, 1949.

Foy, John Vail. "Character and Structure in Edwin Arlington Robinson's Major Narratives." Cornell, 1961.

Fryxell, Lucy D. "Edwin Arlington Robinson as Dramatist and Poet." University of Kentucky, 1955.

Mitchell, George. "Robinson's Sonnets." Temple University, 1949.

Moon, Elmer Samuel. "Organic Form in the Short Poems of Edwin Arlington Robinson." University of Michigan, 1957.

Morrill, Paul Hamilton. "Psychological Aspects of the Poetry of Edwin Arlington Robinson." Northwestern University, 1957.

Perrine, Laurence D. "Edwin Arlington Robinson and the Arthurian Legend." Yale University, 1948.

Stephens, Alan Archer, Jr. "The Shorter Narrative Poems of Edwin Arlington Robinson." University of Missouri, 1954.

Stevick, Robert David. "Edwin Arlington Robinson: The Principles and Practices of His Poetry." University of Wisconsin, 1956.

General Index

167

Index to Robinson's Works